The West Highland Way

Official Guide

SEVENTH EDITION

*Revised and updated by
Roger Smith from an original text
by Bob Aitken*

*Foreword by John Markland, CBE,
Chairman, Scottish Natural Heritage*

**SCOTTISH
NATURAL
HERITAGE**

MERCAT
PRESS

First published in 1980 by HMSO
Second, third and fourth editions published by HMSO
Fifth and sixth editions published by Mercat Press

This seventh edition published in 2004 by Mercat Press
10 Coates Crescent, Edinburgh EH3 7AL
www.mercatpress.com

**SCOTTISH
NATURAL
HERITAGE**

Scottish Natural Heritage is a government agency, established
in April 1992, which works to conserve and enhance Scotland's
natural heritage — the wildlife, habitats and landscapes which
have evolved in Scotland through the long partnership
between people and nature. SNH aims to develop active
partnerships to help people enjoy the natural heritage
responsibly, understand it more fully and use it wisely so it
can be sustained for the future.

*Further information about Scottish Natural Heritage is available
from the Public Relations Office, SNH, 12 Hope Terrace, Edinburgh
EH9 2AS. Tel: 0131 447 4784. Website: www.snh.org.uk*

ISBN: 184183 0666

Printed in HongKong through World Print Ltd

Contents

Foreword

by John Markland, CBE,
Chairman, Scottish Natural Heritage

WHEN it was formally opened in 1980, the West Highland Way became the first officially designated Long Distance Route in Scotland. Since then, it has been enjoyed by tens of thousands of walkers every year. They have followed this challenging route from its starting point in Milngavie, on the outskirts of Glasgow, through the dramatic transition from lowland to highland scenery, to its northern terminus in Fort William at the foot of Scotland's highest mountain.

The popularity of the Way demands constant attention and investment to keep the path at the high standard expected by walkers of such an important route. As Chairman of Scottish Natural Heritage, I am delighted that there is such a willing partnership of local authorities and other bodies working, with our support, to manage and maintain the route for walkers. Working closely together we recognised that after over twenty years of use, considerable investment was needed to improve the condition of the path and to keep it in a good walkable condition in the future. I am pleased to report that a major three year programme of path improvements is nearing completion and I hope the benefits will be evident to you when you walk the route. Funding secured from the Lottery Sports Fund and the European Union has been essential to enable us to undertake this work. It is also good to know that a proportion of the royalties from the sale of this Guide will help directly towards the costs of upkeep of the Way.

The family of Long Distance Routes is still growing. At the time of writing, an extension to the Speyside Way has just been opened, providing a route all the way from Buckie to Aviemore. The Great Glen Way is also now open, and walkers can continue if they wish from the West Highland Way, through Fort William, up the Great Glen Way for 110km/69 miles to Inverness — now there's an even greater challenge.

In this new edition of the Guide, Roger Smith has made

an excellent job of updating the information which is so helpful both for those who wish to walk the whole route in a single journey and for those who are content to spend a day or weekend walking along sections of the route. However you choose to walk the route, I hope you will find this Guide a useful and informative companion to your trip.

Acknowledgements

THE development of long distance routes in Scot land has not been without controversy, but as the routes have matured they have catered for an ever growing number of walkers, bringing enjoyment to many and economic benefits to rural communities. As the first long distance route in Scotland, the West Highland Way has served as a flagship for the network, and it remains the most popular, catering for an estimated 50,000 walkers per annum. Scottish Natural Heritage (SNH) remains indebted to all those who assisted in its development including proprietors and their agents, estate workers and Forestry Commission staff, local authority officials and local people along the route. Since being officially opened in 1980, the Way has been well served by its countryside rangers and by its managing authorities, the Loch Lomond & Trossachs Interim Committee on behalf of Highland Council, Stirling Council, Argyll & Bute Council and East Dunbartonshire Council.

The first edition of this guide, published in 1980, was compiled and written by Robert Aitken who in addition to undertaking the exhaustive background research which led to the guide's informative and amusing historical and anecdotal evidence, also spent many fine and not so fine days walking the route. It is to his credit that so little of his original text has had to be amended in preparing this and the previous revised editions; changes have largely been confined to factual matters where the line of the Way has been altered or where village services have expanded in response to the number of walkers.

Every effort has been made to make the information as up-to-date and practical as possible, but changes will inevitably occur.

In the period in which the Way has been in existence, the managing authorities and SNH (and SNH's predecessor, the Countryside Commission for Scotland) have gained much useful information and opinion from those who have walked the route. Occasional surveys have been undertaken to gauge levels of use, expenditure patterns and, most importantly, walkers' enjoyment of the route and how they consider it could be improved. The many letters received with praise or criticism of the Way have also been appreciated, and we take this opportunity to invite readers to comment on the route or on this guide. Only through your comments will the managing authorities be able, with our support, to improve the management and services along the Way.

> *Scottish Natural Heritage,*
> *Caspian House,*
> *Mariner Court,*
> *Clydebank,*
> *Glasgow G81 2NR.*

Or you can send comments by email to:

info@west-highland-way.co.uk

The publishers' thanks are due to SNH and the Countryside Rangers for their help in checking the text and mapping; and to the following for use of photographs: Lorne Gill of SNH, Alan Forbes, Charles Gulland, Angus McKinnon, Debbie Pope, Roger Smith and Erl B. Wilkie.

The Clyde, Kelvin and Allander Walkways

THESE three linked paths provide a pleasant walking route from the centre of Glasgow to the official start of the West Highland Way at Milngavie, an alternative to taking the train. The route is about 19km in length and is waymarked throughout. There are numerous points of access along the way.

From the city centre, make your way down to the river and turn west. The Clyde Walkway passes the Finnieston Crane and the Scottish Exhibition and Conference Centre before meeting the Kelvin, where the route turns north.

Little remains of the once-great shipbuilding industry on the Clyde, where so many superb ships were launched. The river was originally much wider than it is today, and was contained by a major piece of civil engineering in the 18th and 19th centuries. The Finnieston crane, affectionately known as Big Finn, remains to remind us of the tremendous achievements of the past.

The walkway passes close to the Kelvin Hall, where Glasgow's Transport Museum is housed; the Kelvingrove Art Galleries and Museum, home to many important collections; Kelvingrove Park; Glasgow University; and the Botanic Gardens, with the fairytale Kibble Palace.

Further north the walkway passes through Maryhill and crosses the line of the Antonine Wall, built by the Romans in AD 142, at about the site of the Brasher Bridge, which was constructed with substantial financial assistance from the Chris Brasher Trust.

Shortly after this, as the Kelvin turns east, the route swings west along the Allander Water, which rises in the Kilpatrick Hills and runs for about 9km to its confluence with the Kelvin. The walkway continues to Milngavie Station, where the West Highland Way can be picked up.

The walkways have been developed by Strathclyde Regional Council, Bearsden & Milngavie District Council and the City of Glasgow District Council with assistance from the European Regional Development Fund. A leaflet giving fuller details is available at tourist information centres and other local outlets.

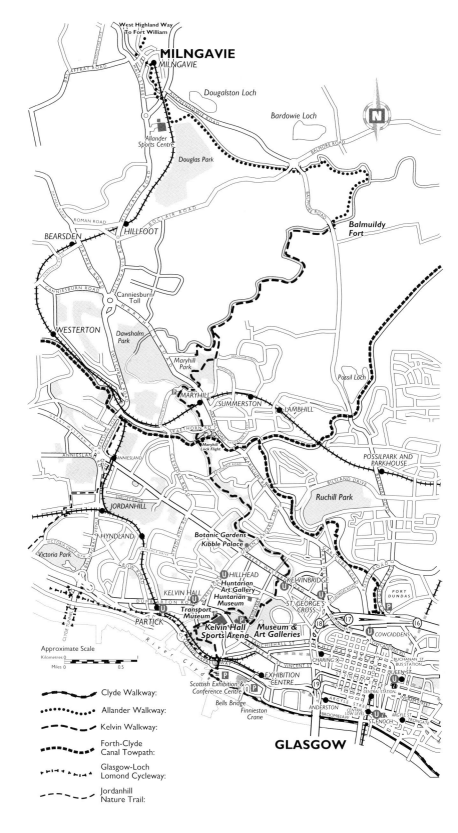

West Highland Way
To Fort William

MILNGAVIE
MILNGAVIE

Dougalston Loch

Bardowie Loch

N

Allander
Sports Centre

Douglas Park

ROMAN ROAD

BEARSDEN HILLFOOT

Balmuildy Fort

CANNIESBURN ROAD

Canniesburn
Toll

WESTERTON

Dawsholm Park

Maryhill Park

Possil Loch

MARYHILL

SUMMERSTON LAMBHILL

ANNIESLAND

Maryhill
Lock Flight

POSSILPARK AND PARKHOUSE

JORDANHILL

BILSLAND DRIVE

Ruchill Park

HYNDLAND

Victoria Park

Botanic Gardens
Kibble Palace

PORT DUNDAS

HILLHEAD
Huntarian
Art Gallery
Huntarian
Museum

KELVINBRIDGE

ST GEORGE'S CROSS

COWCADDENS

CLYDE TUNNEL

KELVIN HALL

Transport
Museum

PARTICK

**Kelvin Hall
Sports Arena**

Museum & Art Galleries

CHARING X

BUCHANAN ST
BUS STATION

QUEEN ST

River Clyde

Approximate Scale
Kilometres 0
Miles 0   0.5

EXHIBITION
CENTRE

CENTRAL STATION

Scottish Exhibition &
Conference Centre

Bells Bridge

*Finnieston
Crane*

ANDERSTON

CENTRAL
LOW LEVEL

ARGYLE ST

ST ENOCH

ARGYLE STREET

BROOMIELAW

TRONGATE

GLASGOW

Clyde Walkway:

Allander Walkway:

Kelvin Walkway:

Forth-Clyde
Canal Towpath:

Glasgow-Loch
Lomond Cycleway:

Jordanhill
Nature Trail:

Walking the Way

T HIS section deals with the practicalities of walking the West Highland Way, and gives general advice to supplement the route description in the main part of the guide. Much of this material will be thoroughly familiar to Scottish walkers and to experienced long-distance walkers in general, but others may have less idea of what to expect on the Way and how to prepare for it. It will do no harm to emphasise at the outset that the West Highland Way is by no means a ramble; while many sections are straightforward walking on excellent, well-drained paths, some parts are gloriously rough and will make for much slower progress. There are stretches which, by British standards, are remote not just from human habitation but from any form of shelter; and the Way is liable to get more than a fair share of wet and windy weather, even in midsummer. Walkers tackling the whole route must realistically expect to have at least some wet going both overhead and underfoot.

Please note that the West Highland Way is a long distance *footpath*, and many sections are not open to mountain bikes, making it inappropriate as a cycle route.

Direction and season

If you wish to tackle the Way as a complete trip, we strongly recommend that you walk south to north, from Milngavie to Fort William; the guide has been written with this assumption in mind. At the simplest level — and this also applies to those walking short sections of the Way — as you head northwards you will have the sun at your back, rather than in your eyes, and are more likely to have wind and rain behind you, or on your left flank, than in your face. The stages between accommodation and supply points are longer, and there is more uphill work, on the northern part of the Way, so that the southern start offers a gentler 'warm-up'. Above all, however, the northwards journey has a greater aesthetic appeal, in its progression from the urban through the domestic and pastoral to the wild mountain and moorland country, and in the scenic crescendo of the last quarter north of Kingshouse where the switchback from ridgecrest to valley creates a vivid sense of mountain travel. The opposite progression from north to south has its own attractions, but inevitably lacks that positive climax.

Try to avoid the peak summer months of July and August if at all possible. It is true these can normally be expected to be the warmest time of the year, but they are not the driest, and hot weather often brings a heavy, enervating mugginess with haze obscuring distant views. There is much to recommend May and June, usually the months of lowest rainfall in West Scotland and often blessed with settled periods of warm dry weather, with diamond-sharp visibility and 18 hours or more of daylight. These months, with April, are also among the best for the naturalist, since spring flowers are in bloom and birds are nesting, while the tree canopy is still relatively open and does not inhibit bird-watching as it can do later. The bracken which in autumn can tower over head-height on open slopes is still low and freshly green, and midges are less of a nuisance. In the mountain country, there may well still be a lingering wreath of snow on the tops to sharpen the line of ridge and corrie.

It is worth noting here that the long-established Scottish Six-Day Motor Cycle Trials are held in the first week of May each year, with several hundred machines taking part. The event often uses sections of the Way between Bridge of Orchy and Fort William, and the latter town, as the event headquarters, is very busy with bikes, riders, support teams and followers. The event is a remarkable spectacle, but walkers wishing to avoid the disturbance of the bikes can get advice from the Ranger Service in Glen Nevis (details on page *xxix*) or from the trail website, *www.west-highland-way.co.uk*.

July and August are the high tourist season in the Highlands generally, and as well as larger numbers on the Way, there will be heavy traffic on many of the roads along or adjoining the route, and corresponding pressure on accommodation. Hotels may be fully booked and bed and breakfast places are often taken up fairly early in the day, particularly in bad weather, when you might be most inclined to look for a roof over your head. While such potential difficulties can be avoided by booking ahead, they do reduce your freedom to change plans in response to weather or personal inclination.

Accommodation difficulties lessen during the autumn, which has the added splendour of changing colours in farmland, woodland and moorland: late September and October will usually see the finest effects. Undeniably there is a higher risk of wet and windy conditions, or of calm, midge-ridden evenings, but the first frosts will decimate the midges and can bring glowing days of un-blemished clarity and rich colour. Winter can be grim or glorious, sodden wet or snow-blanketed, gale-swept or frost-bound; and again accommodation can become a problem as some hotels, hostels and bed and breakfast places are closed.

Following the Way

The West Highland Way has been comprehensively but unobtrusively marked on the ground by the managing authorities, using standard signposts and waymark posts to the Scottish Natural Heritage specification. All the waymarkers can readily be identified by their dark brown colour-stain and by the SNH long-distance footpath symbol, a thistle within a hexagon. Signposts and waymark posts with yellow arrows are found where the Way changes course. Confirmation markers bearing the symbol alone show the line of the Way where, for ex-ample, it passes a junction of paths without turning, or where it crosses open fields or moorland without any other directional aids, such as a fence or a dyke, to follow.

The general waymarking policy has been to keep the number of markers to a minimum consistent with safe route-finding. Thus there are fewer markers on sections where the line of the route is already clear, as on forest roads or along the shore of Loch Lomond. The Way is marked in detail on Ordnance Survey maps and on the special 1:40,000 map sheet prepared by Harveys to accom-pany this guide, and reference to the map should clear up any difficulties.

The longitudinal 'shape' of the West Highland Way presented an awkward problem of mapping, which has been cleverly resolved by the use of a long strip of map divided into sections. This avoids the need to insert a large number of map pages in the guide, or to purchase five standard OS 1:50,000 Landranger sheets (64, 57, 56, 50 and 41) or seven 1:25,000 Explorer maps (342, 347, 348, 364, 377, 384 and 392). The special map clearly covers a limited corridor of country, and should of course be supplemented by the appropriate Landranger or Explorer sheet if you are moving off the line of the Way, to climb a particular hill, for example.

Times and distances

The guide avoids any detailed suggestion of timing for the route. Every party will be different in composition and fitness, in interests and inclinations, and in the weight of the packs its members carry. Weather, underfoot conditions and length of daylight are extra variables to be considered. There is nothing worse than to feel constrained, however subconsciously, by someone else's idea of how long it should take to cover a given distance.

Most walkers attempting the whole Way will be able to complete the distance in a week; this gives an average of about 21 km (13 miles) a day — and a user survey showed that the normal time taken was, in fact, six or seven days. Those who view it as an athletic excursion rather than an aesthetic one can obviously do it much faster; on the other hand it would be perfectly possible to spend a fortnight or more along the West Highland Way, particularly if you take the opportunity to explore the country around it, and to climb some of the grand hills that overlook it.

Much of the Way gives easy walking in good conditions, on old-established footpaths, forest roads, historic military roads, and former railway lines. On these sections you can make a rough estimate of the time required for the distance by using Naismith's Rule, named after its originator who was one of the heroes of early mountaineering in Scotland, a founder of the Scottish Mountaineering Club, and a prodigious walker himself. The rule allows one hour for every 5 km (3 miles) on the flat, with an additional half-hour for each 300m (1000 feet) of climbing. Extra allowance should be made for heavy packs or poor conditions.

This guide divides the Way into eight sections accessible by public road at either end. If you are tackling the route in short stretches, you should find that these sections break the Way up into convenient stages; if you are backpacking, you will make your own stages in response to weather conditions and your needs for accommodation and services.

Accommodation

Given that the West Highland Way passes through a good deal of sparsely-populated country, there is an adequate supply of accessible accommodation along its length, but not so much that it can be taken for granted. As already mentioned, in the high season there is pressure on all forms of accommodation, while in the off season some of it closes down.

Detailed information, including phone numbers, is provided in the Way information leaflet prepared by the Way's managing authorities, and available from them, from Scottish Natural Heritage or from local tourist information centres. You should always check accommodation details in advance, as local circumstances can change quite rapidly. Addresses for tourist boards and information centres along the Way are given at the end of this section.

The 'Walkers Welcome' Scheme

Scottish Natural Heritage and VisitScotland promote a scheme whereby accommodation establishments can, if they wish, display a 'Walkers Welcome' symbol in their windows. This indicates that the proprietors are willing to cater for the particular needs of walkers, and should ensure a warm welcome. In return, walkers are asked to consider the needs of the proprietors and of other guests.

Please bear in mind that many establishments along the Way cater for visitors whose needs differ from walkers. Not everyone will readily tolerate the problems caused by bulky, wet packs and muddy boots! The Walkers Welcome scheme should mean that courteous walkers get a courteous welcome.

Hotels and Guest Houses

Hotel accommodation is available at regular intervals, but many of the hotels are small, or cater for a specialised clientele such as fishermen; so it is sensible — especially in summer — to book in advance if possible. The Way information leaflet has all the necessary details for hotels on the route; the VisitScotland guide, *Where to Stay in Scotland: Hotels and Guest Houses,* lists other hotels in the wider area around the Way. It is published annually and is available from VisitScotland at 23 Ravelston Terrace, Edinburgh EH4 3EU (0845 2255 121, *www.visitscotland.com*).

Bed and Breakfast is offered in a fair number of private houses along the Way, especially in the villages. Inevitably, however, there is little accommodation of this type between Rowardennan and Crianlarich, simply because the country is so thinly populated. The Crianlarich-Tyndrum area and Kinlochleven are well provided, but a long way apart. Much of the bed-and-breakfast trade is casual, so walkers must compete with other visitors, but you can book ahead using the information in the Way accommodation leaflet. You can keep your schedule flexible by telephoning in the morning to reserve accommodation for that evening.

It may also be possible to hire a static caravan for a night on one of the caravan sites by the Way, particularly outside the peak season.

It is worth noting here that mobile phone coverage of the area cannot be guaranteed, due to the nature of the terrain, and therefore should not be relied on as the sole means of communication.

Hostels

The Scottish Youth Hostels Association has three hostels on the Way. Rowardennan is open March-October; Crianlarich is open February-October and winter weekends; and Glen Nevis is open all year. These are available only to members of Youth Hostel associations, but it is possible to join the SYHA at any of the hostels. At all three it is advisable to book accommodation for Easter, July and August, and other holiday weekends. Full details of membership, and the current leaflet, can be obtained by writing to the national office: SYHA, 7 Glebe Crescent, Stirling FK8 2JA (*www.syha.org.uk*).

Bunkhouses and Private Hostels

Bunkhouses offer a similar range of facilities to those provided in youth hostels, at equivalent prices. In many cases these form part of a larger facility, such as an hotel or restaurant, offering additional services including meals and refreshments. Space can be limited, so it is advisable to book in advance at peak periods. There are bunkhouses at Balmaha, Tyndrum, Kingshouse, Kinlochleven, Fort William and Glen Nevis. There is also a bunkhouse at the Bridge of Orchy Hotel, although at present there are no self-catering facilities. Bar meals are available in the hotel.

Some of these bunkhouses are part of the growing network of private hostels in Scotland. For a full list of these hostels, write to IBH Scotland, Fraoch Lodge Hostel, Boat of Garten PH24 3BN, enclosing an A5 size stamped and addressed reply envelope. There is a website listing independent hostels at *www.hostel-scotland.co.uk.*

Wigwams

A number of 'wigwam' shelters have been provided along the Way. These intriguing wooden structures offer simple accommodation in the form of a sleeping platform but no other facilities, but all are sited on farms. The wigwams, which sleep up to 6 people, can be pre-booked, and a modest charge is made for their use. You will find them at Easter Druimquhassle Farm near Drymen; Beinglas Farm, Glen Falloch; and Auchtertyre Farm in Strath Fillan. For details see the Way information leaflet or the website.

Camping

Without doubt camping is the most free and flexible mode of accommodation for any long-distance walker; it liberates you from the ties of pre-booked lodgings, and lets you go or stay as weather or fancy dictate. On the other hand, camping implies gear and hence a much heavier pack: the West Highland Way calls for a modern, waterproof tent with flysheet and a good sleeping bag. Camping also brings more intimate contact with the natural environment, and a greater responsibility to care for it.

Advice on camping along the Way is contained in the information leaflet and on the website. Basically, you should only camp on recognised sites or on the designated informal backpacking sites which are listed in the information leaflet and shown on the map. Otherwise, you should always ask permission before camping, especially in the vicinity of dwellings, and should observe the Country Code with great care. The aim should always be to leave your site with no sign that you have been there.

Sanitary arrangements are especially important. If you need a latrine, dig a hole well away from your campsite and a good distance from any watercourse to avoid the risk of pollution. Cover the waste matter and burn any toilet paper used. A useful leaflet, *Where to 'Go' in the Great Outdoors*, is available free from the Mountaineering Council of Scotland, as is an advice leaflet on wild camping.

Services and supplies

The route description in the guide gives a general outline of the service facilities and shops available on and near the Way. You should note before setting off that there is no centre with a population of over 2000 between Milngavie and Fort William, and that there are only small villages between Drymen and Kinlochleven. Don't expect shops in these places to hold large or specialised stocks: plan your supplies in advance.

In the table opposite the settlements are listed from south to north along the Way. Settlements actually on the Way are in italics; all the others are within easy walking distance.

Managing the Way

A heavily-used route such as the West Highland Way demands a considerable management effort to keep it at the quality demanded by walkers, and some notes on the current management regime operating along the Way may be of interest.

The Way is primarily managed by the ranger services attached to the Loch Lomond & Trossachs National Park (based at Balmaha) and to Highland Regional Council (based in Glen Nevis). These rangers also work on behalf

	eating places	food shop	post office[1]	bank	doctor	police	tourist information centre
Milngavie	●	●	●	●	●	●	
Strathblane	●	●	●	●	●	●	
Killearn	●	●	●	●	●	●	
Drymen	●	●	●	●	●	●	●
Balmaha	●	●					
Cashel		●[2]					
Rowardennan	●	●[3]					
Inversnaid	●						
Ardlui	●	●	●				
Crianlarich	●	●	●				
Tyndrum	●	●	●				●
Bridge of Orchy	●						
Kingshouse	●						
Kinlochleven	●	●	●	●	●	●	●
Fort William	●	●	●	●	●	●	●

1 Only in the larger villages do post offices offer a Savings Bank facility.
2 The shop in the campsite at Cashel opens seasonally with the campsite.
3 The store in the Youth Hostel (when open) might supply food to non-hostellers in need.

of the local authorities along the route. There are also National Trust for Scotland rangers at Ben Lomond and in Glencoe, and Blackmount Estate has a ranger.

Walkers may also see maintenance wardens out on the route. They try to keep abreast of any work required, but they and the rangers are always grateful for reports of damage to trail infrastructure, etc. Please be specific if you make such a report — it is frustrating to be told that 'there's a stile broken near Tyndrum' as this could cover a substantial area!

The revenue cost for maintenance is currently (2004) about £150,000 per year. This covers replacement of worn-out, broken or damaged items such as stiles, gates and footbridges; interpretive signs; waymarks and finger-posts; and Way 'furniture' generally.

A major upgrading programme of work along the Way, costing over £500,000, has recently been completed. This work (funded by the Lottery Sports Fund, Scottish Natural Heritage and grants from Europe) has included surface improvements, rerouting, replacing stiles with kissing gates as appropriate, improving ancillary signage, and upgrading the interpretation.

It is fair to say that the going for walkers has improved considerably over the past 20 years. Walkers using this guidebook are helping; a percentage of the proceeds from sales is used as a contribution towards the maintenance of the route.

Charity Events and Races

A popular route such as the West Highland Way is bound to attract organised events, and it is possible, especially in summer, that you might encounter participants in one of these.

The largest current annual event is the Caledonian Challenge, which takes place in June. It involves teams walking or running 54 miles of the route (Fort William to Inverarnan) and raising substantial sums for designated charities. In 2003 the event attracted 1500 walkers plus support teams, marshals, etc. There is also an annual West Highland Way race. The current record time for the complete Way is an astonishing 15½ hours.

Transport

Since the West Highland Way follows a relatively low-level route through hill country, it tends to parallel the main lines of road and rail communication and is rarely far from them. As a result it is quite possible, with a little planning, to walk the Way in short sections using public transport to return to a base or to the starting point. The guide is divided into a series of such sections, ending at points accessible by public road; at the end of each section an outline is given of the means of transport available there.

As far as Balmaha the Way is never more than a short distance from a bus route; from Inverarnan northwards it runs roughly parallel with the West Highland Railway to Bridge of Orchy, and with the A82 road to Kingshouse Hotel at the head of Glencoe. On Loch Lomond during the summer, occasional ferry services provide cross-links to the west shore, and from Balloch to Inversnaid, calling at Luss and Rowardennan (see end of section for further details).

Naturally, since much of the country of the Way is sparsely populated, most of the train and bus services are not frequent, even in summer: two or three services per day is about normal. Timetables change from year to year and you should check the current position in Glasgow at the transport terminals or the Information Centre in George Square, or in Fort William at the travel centre north of the town centre.

Weather

The West Highland Way runs in and over mountain country on the west side of Scotland, so almost by definition it is subject to very changeable weather at any time of year, and particularly to windy and wet conditions. In general terms, rainfall increases as the Way goes north and as it climbs to higher altitudes. Thus, while the average annual rainfall in the Glasgow area is around 1000 mm (40 inches), and is not a great deal higher at the southern end of Loch Lomond, by the head of the loch it has risen to twice that figure. The mountains west of Rannoch Moor, in Glen Coe, and above Kinlochleven have rainfall levels approaching that recorded on Ben Nevis, well over 3000 mm (100 inches). By way of consolation the valleys are slightly drier; Kinlochleven and Fort William each record around 2000 mm (80 inches). West Highland rainfall has what the meteorologists call 'a low coefficient of variation' which means it is unlikely to be much more or less than the average in any given year.

As a rule, about five-eighths of this precipitation falls during the winter half of the year, so a good deal of it is in the form of snow. In a normal year snow covers the summit of Ben Nevis for all but 75 days, and lingers into May on many of the mountains by the Way. Below 300 metres (1000 feet) snow is unlikely to lie for more than 30 days in total.

This reflects the relative mildness of the weather on the whole. Summer average temperatures are not high — the typical July figure is around 13°—15°C (the upper 50s F) — and these fall quite quickly with altitude, but winter averages and extremes are less cold than further east towards the centre of Scotland. January average temperatures near sea level will usually be 3°—4°C (up to 6°—8°F) above freezing.

The walker's real enemy is wind, particularly in combination with rain or snow. South-westerlies predominate.
Wind-speed rises markedly with altitude: Glasgow gets
about six days with gales a year, Ben Nevis about fifty.
The higher stretches of the Way tend to be bare and open
and are thus exposed to the full force of the wind. Wind
and rain together in these circumstances make for a risk
of exposure, and you should know and watch for the
symptoms in all members of the party.

Gales can strike at any time of the year. As far as other
weather conditions are concerned, early summer has already been recommended. In a normal year April, May
and June will be the driest months in the country around
the Way, usually getting less than 20% of the annual rainfall between them. August may be very wet; at Fort
William on average almost twice as much rain falls in
August as in May. As a corollary of this, May is generally
the sunniest month of the year, enjoying about a sixth of
the year's total hours of bright sunshine. Nevertheless, it
is usually 4°—5°C (about 8°F) cooler than the warmest
month, July.

Particularly at higher levels along the Way the weather
can change with startling speed from good to bad or vice
versa. This should be borne in mind when pitching camp,
or when setting off on one of the upland sections of the
route. In doubtful conditions it may be helpful (if you
can) to phone the Glasgow Weather Centre (0141 248
3451) for a local forecast, or listen to BBC Radio Scotland
(92—95 FM or 810 medium wave).

The managing authorities have tried to take account of
all weather conditions in preparing the Way, particularly
in providing footbridges on burns, but in extreme
weather even a tiny burn may become a fearsome tor-
rent. Such exceptional conditions rarely last long and it
is generally wiser to retreat and wait out foul weather in
shelter rather than risk a soaking or even a drowning.
On the other hand it is not a good idea to wait for mist to
clear from high ground. Cloud can cling to the hills for
days on end. A party that lacks the ability to find its way
in mist should not venture on the upland stretches of the
West Highland Way.

Equipment

The West Highland Way is essentially a long hill-walking expedition, and unless you plan only to take a short walk over the more domestic sections south of Drymen, you should equip yourself as for hill-walking.

Starting from the ground, a pair of walking boots, with moulded or cleated soles, are basic items. Trainers or walking shoes invite wet feet and would be a liability on the rougher parts of the route: wellington boots are certainly quite appropriate on some sections, but would be risky on others, and are rarely comfortable over any long distance. Anklets or gaiters are useful over boots at any time of year to keep out water, snow or mud.

Trousers or breeches are very much a matter for personal preference; shorts can be carried as an option but it would be folly to wear them as the only form of leg covering. Waterproof trousers are very useful. The usual 'top' of a light, warm shirt and sweater or fleece — with a spare in the rucksack — should be augmented by one or more outer layers, such as an anorak and/or cagoule, the combination being both windproof and waterproof. Gloves or mitts, and a balaclava or woolly hat, should be carried at all seasons. The phrase 'it can be winter any day of the year on the Scottish hills' may be hackneyed, but it is true.

Equipment should also include the usual safeguards and routefinding aids — map, compass, torch and whistle; some emergency food; and a small first-aid kit: even one or two roller bandages can be invaluable in case of an accident. Midge repellent is recommended between June and mid-October. Plastic bags are useful. A big one can double as an inner waterproof lining for the rucksack and an emergency bivvy bag, while smaller ones can keep individual items like spare clothing and food dry and separate from one another. They are invaluable for campers, not least in keeping order in a cluttered tent.

In winter or early spring an ice-axe is a vital item if you mean to tackle any of the mountains around the route and should be complemented by rope and crampons for any but the easiest ascents.

If you wish to camp, your load will be a good deal

heavier and a comfortable well-packed rucksack is of prime importance. Since nights can be chilly even in summer, a good quality sleeping bag is a great comfort. As already suggested, a tent without a flysheet on the West Highland Way is asking for trouble; and you must carry your own stove.

Training and Preparation

Particularly if you are unaccustomed to rough walking or to carrying a substantial pack, it will pay dividends in enjoyment to undertake a bit of preparatory training for the Way. Every opportunity should be taken to work up the walking muscles; new gear — especially boots or pack — should be well broken in; and the equipment to be carried should be ruthlessly reviewed to cut down on weight.

From the experiences of walkers surveyed on the Way, a few practical points of advice may be useful:

— carry the absolute minimum of gear commensurate with being adequately equipped. You should never carry more than a third of your own weight, and for comfort 10 kilos (22 lbs) would be a desirable target weight;

— don't rush at the Way, especially if you are not fully fit. If you overdo it on the first day, it may take most of the rest of the Way to recover;

— attend to blisters, ankle chafing and other foot problems as soon as you become aware of them;

— if in doubt about the line of the Way, sit down and work it out from map and guide, rather than pushing on hopefully and possibly in the wrong direction.

Pests

At any time between May and October, insect pests can be a nuisance. In the earlier part of the season, clegs (horse-flies) can give a nasty bite; later on, sheep-ticks may be a problem — you should avoid sitting in deep grass or bracken, particularly if you are wearing shorts.

Clegs and ticks seem to have good and bad years, but

midges are never in short supply. Clouds of these tiny stinging insects can make camping, or even stopping for a few minutes, a purgatorial experience, especially in July and August. They are most active in calm, warm and humid conditions; fortunately even a light breeze will keep them down. It is well worth bearing this in mind when selecting a campsite.

If you are walking the Way in high summer, you may well find that a good insect repellent is worth its weight in gold. Repellent 'candles', for burning inside a tent, are also available. It is best — though far from easy — to abstain from scratching midge-bites, as they subside quickly; but if you are sensitive to insect bites, you should carry an appropriate lotion to treat them.

Going on the Hills

One of the particular attractions of the West Highland Way is that it passes close by many striking and attractive hills. You may well be keen to tackle a few of these, and the guide outlines some suggestions for ways up the most obvious peaks. However, bad weather can strike suddenly to turn even the simplest climb, on paths like those on Ben Lomond or Ben Nevis, into a serious and potentially dangerous expedition. Although there are straightforward routes on most of the hills around the Way, many of them are bounded by steep, broken corries or crags; and to go astray on the ridges can bring a party down into remote and pathless country on the wrong side of the hill.

You should, therefore, prepare for any climbs that appeal to you by having a good look at the appropriate OS Landranger or Explorer map sheet, and by consulting guide books. The series of regional guides produced by the Scottish Mountaineering Club can be recommended, but there are plenty of other excellent sources. The wider background knowledge gained in this way brings an extra enjoyment to days on the hill. You must also consider whether your proposed climb will interfere with deer-stalking or lambing (see the later sections in this chapter).

You are strongly advised to read, and heed, the advice contained in the Mountain Code for Scotland:

Before you go–

> Learn the use of map and compass
> Know the weather signs and local forecast
> Plan within your capabilities
> Know simple first aid and the symptoms of exposure
> Know the mountain distress signals
> Know the Country Code

When you go–

> Think carefully before you go alone
> Leave written word of your route and report your
>   return
> Take windproofs, woollens and survival bag
> Take map, compass, torch and food
> Wear proper hillwalking boots
> Keep alert all day

In winter–

> Always have an ice axe for each person
> Carry a climbing rope and know the correct use of
>   rope and ice axe
> Learn to recognise dangerous snow slopes.

In the Countryside

Walkers on the West Highland Way have a special responsibility to conduct themselves carefully and thoughtfully in the countryside. Because you are following a confined route, your impacts are concentrated; because you are walking what was the first of Scotland's long distance footpaths, you are creating an impression, favourable or otherwise, which may affect the future of such routes.

The 12 points of the Country Code, which provide excellent guidance for behaviour in the countryside generally, can be amplified for the particular case of the Way:

1 　*Guard against all risk of fire*

The West Highland Way passes through considerable tracts of woodland, both semi-natural and planted, which contribute a great deal to the scenic value of the route apart from their intrinsic ecological and economic worth. The greatest care should be taken to avoid accidental fire and you should not make campfires at all. Even on peat moorland campfires pose a risk of widespread damage and leave an unsightly scar. As a sign in the Doire Darach pinewood at Loch Tulla puts it: 'that which burns never returns'.

2   *Leave all gates as you find them*

If a farmer has left a gate open, it is for a good reason such as moving stock from one field to another. However, if you find a gate shut you should *always* close it firmly behind you.

3   *Use gates and stiles to cross fences, hedges and walls*

There should be no need to climb over fences or dykes on the Way, as stiles or gates have been provided wherever necessary.

4   *Keep your dog under close control*

The managing authorities recommend that you do not take dogs on the West Highland Way at all. Over substantial lengths of the Way — on Conic Hill, in Glen Falloch, and in Strath Fillan — the access agreement with the proprietor explicitly forbids dogs. On other, rough sections of the route, as on Loch Lomondside, a dog may be a real handicap to the party. More generally, the greater part of the Way runs across land used for grazing sheep and cattle; if dogs must be taken they should be kept on a lead to avoid any risk or suspicion that they may worry the stock.

5   *Keep to public paths across farmland*

The West Highland Way is a defined and agreed route, and there should be no need to wander away from the route across farmland, whether arable or pasture.

6   *Take your litter home*

Day walkers on the Way should take all their litter home. Long-distance walkers should keep litter until they reach a service centre: bins in roadside lay-bys can become filled to overflowing during the summer season. Both should aim to take away more litter than they themselves brought. Remember that sparsely populated rural areas have limited resources to collect and dispose of other people's rubbish.

7   Help to keep all water clean

A substantial part of the Way passes through water catchment areas ranging in scale from the Loch Lomond basin to small streams supplying single houses. The smaller supplies in particular are not treated and you should be careful to avoid the sort of pollution caused by insanitary arrangements while camping, or by leaving food or other refuse in or close to streams.

8   Protect wildlife, plants and trees

A great part of the Way possesses a high natural history interest, which can best be maintained by not interfering with it. In particular you should not pick flowers, break trees or chase wild animals, all of which will reduce the enjoyment of the Way for future walkers.

9   Take special care on country roads

The Way uses short sections of rural road where an alternative off-road route is not available. For your own safety you should take particular care on these roads, many of which are narrow, winding and hilly but can nevertheless be very busy in the tourist season. Walk to face the oncoming traffic, and in poor light or darkness carry a torch or wear light-coloured clothing.

10   Enjoy the countryside and respect its life and work

11   Make no unnecessary noise

The Way passes through a number of small communities and close to many individual farms, lodges and private houses. It is good manners to respect the property and privacy of local residents, and to avoid disturbing them with noise.

12   Leave livestock, crops and machinery alone

The southern part of the Way passes through prosperous farmland, with arable crops and livestock rearing, where the need to protect these productive activities is obvious. The rough grazing and deer forest of the Highland part of the Way, though less intensively used, also contributes to agricultural production and rural employment. Two countryside concerns in that area must be specifically mentioned:

Deer-stalking and Lambing

The Scottish Highlands hold a large red deer population, representing not only a superb feature of local wildlife but a valuable economic resource. Since they have no natural predators, the adult deer must be culled to maintain a healthy population and to reduce their impact on agricultural land. Thus the sport of deer-stalking is at once a recreation, a valuable form of tourism, and an ecological necessity. It provides employment and helps to conserve the rural environment.

Stag stalking is largely carried out between mid-August and late October. Walkers can cause direct disturbance to deer which makes the stalking more difficult. During this critical period walkers should consider how they can minimise any disturbance. The Hillphones service provides daily updates (by recorded message) on stalking activities in the Highlands, and how these might affect walkers. The relevant numbers are: Glen Falloch 01499 600137; Glen Dochart 01567 820886; Grey Corries/Mamores 01855 831511.

The safe and courteous course for walkers is to stay on the line of the Way, especially on higher ground. If you are keen to have a day on the hills, seek permission locally. As long as walkers show consideration for their interests, most deer forest proprietors will try to offer an alternative route that will not clash with their own activity.

It is worth noting that there is open access to the mountain land held by the National Trust for Scotland during the stalking season; some of the finest mountain country near the Way, the hills of Glen Coe, is thus accessible all year round, as is Ben Lomond.

For the hill sheep farmer the lambing season, which may run from mid-March to May, is the busiest and most important time in his calendar. During this period dogs should not be taken on to sheep grazings at all. You should try to avoid disturbing pregnant ewes: if surprised and forced to run, they may become distressed and lose their lambs, with a real financial cost to the farmer. Do not pick up lambs that have apparently been abandoned, or try to assist lambing ewes. It is better to report any such animals in distress to the nearest farmer.

As this edition was prepared for press, new access legislation was being considered by the Scottish Parliament. Although this legislation would give a general right of access to all open ground, the advice given above should still be heeded in the interests of maintaining the excellent relationship which currently exists between landowners, farmers and walkers in Scotland.

The National Park

The Loch Lomond and Trossachs National Park, the first of its kind in Scotland, was officially designated in 2002. It covers a wide area stretching from Loch Earn in the east to Cowal in the west and from Balloch up to Crianlarich. There is a park information centre at Balmaha where further information can be found.

The National Park includes a substantial section of the West Highland Way, and the management of this part of the route will be taken over by the Park authorities, working closely with the local authorities and other interested organisations.

Useful Addresses

General Enquiries and Accommodation

VisitScotland (the Scottish Tourist Board), 23 Ravelston Terrace, Edinburgh EH4 3EE (0845 2255 121, *www.visitscotland.com*).

Greater Glasgow and Clyde Valley Tourist Board, 11 George Square, Glasgow G2 1DZ (0141 204 4400, *enquiries@seeglasgow.com*). *Covers Milngavie-Drymen*

Argyll, The Isles, Loch Lomond, Stirling and Trossachs Tourist Board, 41 Dumbarton Road, Stirling FK8 2QQ (08707 200620, *stirlingtic@aillst.ossian.net*). *Covers Drymen-Bridge of Orchy*

The Highlands of Scotland Tourist Board, Cameron Square, Fort William PH33 6AJ (01397 703781, *fortwilliam@host.co.uk*). Tourist Information Centre open all year. *Covers Rannoch Moor-Fort William*

Tourist Information Centre, Drymen Library, The Square, Drymen (08707 200611). Open May-September.

Tourist Information Centre, Main Street, Tyndrum (08707 200626). Open April-October.

There is an excellent trail website giving a great deal of useful information at *www.west-highland-way.co.uk.*

Travel Enquiries

National rail enquiries line: 08457 48 49 50. ScotRail time-table information can be found on *www.scotrail.co.uk.*

Scottish Citylink Coaches, Buchanan Street Bus Station, Buchanan Street, Glasgow G1 (0990 50 50 50 *www.citylink.co.uk*). For bus services from Glasgow to Fort William.

Ferries on Loch Lomond

Rowardennan-Inverbeg: Easter to end September (enquiries: Rowardennan Hotel, 01360 870273).

Inversnaid-Inveruglas: March to December (contact Inversnaid Hotel, 01877 386223).

Ardleish-Ardlui: April-October (contact Ardlui Hotel, 01301 704243).

Tarbert-Rowardennan-Inverbeg (contact Cruise Loch Lomond, 01301 702356).

Weather

Glasgow Weather Centre, 118 Waterloo Street, Glasgow G2 (0141 248 3451). There are regular forecasts on BBC Radio Scotland, 92-95khz FM or 810 on medium wave.

Countryside Ranger Services

Countryside Rangers operate along the Way. As well as footpath monitoring and liaising with other land users, they will gladly provide advice and information to walkers and potential walkers. Contact:

Countryside Ranger Service, Loch Lomond National Park Cantre, Balmaha G63 OJQ (01360 870470, *info@west-highland-way.co.uk*).

Countryside Ranger Service, Highland Council, Ionad Nibheis, Glen Nevis, Fort William PH33 6PF (01397 705922, *ranger@w-high-way-north.demon.co.uk*).

Accommodation booking and luggage carrying

Accommodation booking services for Way-walkers are operated by two companies.

Easyways, Room 32, Haypark Business Centre, Marchmont Avenue, Polmont FK2 ONZ, 01324 714132, email: *info@easyways.com*

AMS, 29 Craigend Road, Condorrat, Glasgow G67 4JX, 01236 722795, email: *info@amstransfers.com*

Luggage carrying services are offered by AMS and also by Travel-Lite, 5 Mugdock Road, Milngavie, Glasgow G62 8PD, 0141 956 7890, email: *info@travel-lite-uk.com*

General advice

Mountaineering Council of Scotland, The Old Granary, West Mill Street, Perth PH1 5QP (01738 638227, *www.mountaineering-scotland.org.uk*)

Walkers' Comments

Scottish Natural Heritage welcomes comments from walkers. If you would like to make any comments on the West Highland Way, please write to Scottish Natural Heritage, Caspian House, Mariner Court, Clydebank Business Park, Clydebank, Glasgow G81 2NR.

Introduction

THE West Highland Way was the first long distance footpath to be established in Scotland under the provisions of the Countryside (Scotland) Act of 1967. The Way runs for 152 km (95 miles) from Milngavie northwards to Fort William — from the outskirts of Scotland's largest city to the foot of its highest mountain, along the shores of its largest loch and across its grandest moor. The West Highland Way is, however, much more than a linking of these topographical superlatives: it is a magnificent walk of very varied character through some of the finest scenery of lowland and highland, mountain and loch, woodland and moorland that Scotland has to show. It provides walking which is in parts pleasant and relaxing, in parts strenuous and rough, in parts remote and exposed to the risk of wild weather.

The Way mirrors the great evolution of landscape taste in the 18th and 19th centuries, to which we owe our present enthusiasm for natural scenery. It moves from the urban and domestic in lowland Central Scotland through the romantic and picturesque in Loch Lomond and Glen Falloch to the savage and sublime in Rannoch and Lochaber. In this passage from Lowlands to Highlands the walker on the Way experiences sharp contrasts in geology and landforms, in flora and fauna, and in the human patterns of land use and settlement. Everywhere in the country around the route there are the traces of human history; history dominated by tensions and conflicts between two cultures, but also coloured by trade and traffic between them.

In fact much of the West Highland Way follows ancient and historic routes. It makes use of the old footpaths of the Highlanders, and the drove roads by which they herded their cattle southwards to Lowland markets in a trade which was still active a century ago. It makes extensive use of the 18th century military roads, built largely by troops to help control the Jacobite clansmen. It uses old coaching roads and farm roads in the Lowlands; and it follows the course of railway lines where trains ran not so very long ago.

Substantial stretches of the Way have always been open to the walker as public rights of way, and have been enjoyed by generations of outdoor enthusiasts; but the virtue of the route's official designation and creation has been to link these together into a coherent entity of great character: the total is considerably more than the sum of its parts. Thus, while many fine short sections are readily accessible by car or by public transport, for maximum enjoyment the West Highland Way should be walked as a whole, or at least in substantial sections. Only by this approach can the walker fully appreciate the wealth of landscape contrast and achieve the genuine sense of travel that the Way offers.

The idea of a long-distance footpath from Glasgow northwards had its origins far back in the Glasgow tramping and climbing tradition; elements of the West Highland Way can be identified in outdoor magazines of the 1930s and 40s. However, the concept of the route began to crystallise in the late 1960s, with Tom Stephenson's Pennine Way in England as a precedent, and the Countryside (Scotland) Act of 1967 as the means of realisation. There was a happy co-ordination of activity between the outdoor interests and government agencies. During 1969 the Glasgow Group of the Holiday Fellowship and other clubs, under the enthusiastic direction of Tom Hunter, undertook much survey work on a potential footpath northwards from Glasgow, while at the end of that year the Scottish Development Department commissioned F.J.Evans to make an examination and report on 'A Footpath System North of Glasgow'. The results of the Glasgow Group's survey were generously made available to Mr Evans, whose report endorsed their proposal for a long-distance route from Glasgow as far as Glen Falloch, the northern half being outwith his immediate remit. He called it 'Highland Footway'.

After considering this report, the Countryside Commission for Scotland decided to investigate the potential route in detail. In 1972, after much fieldwork, the Commission submitted its study report for the route, now called 'The West Highland Way', to the local authorities who would be concerned with its implementation. In the light of its consultations with these authorities, the Commission at the end of 1973 submitted a revised report to the Secretary of State for Scotland for his approval, which was given in September 1974. It is a tribute to the work of the outdoor clubs' working party that the Way was approved very much along the line their survey had suggested.

The implementation of the Way — the negotiation with proprietors over access agreements and the details of the route, the provision of bridges, gates and stiles, waymarking and information boards — was a longer, slower process than anyone would have wished. Soon after the Secretary of State had given his approval, the reorganisation of local government in Scotland transformed the implementing authorities from five old counties into three new Regions — Strathclyde, Central and Highland. Inevitably, considerable changes in organisational structures, areas of responsibility, and staff, led to a loss of continuity and momentum in implementation. Shortly thereafter again, economic cuts reduced the manpower and finance available to carry forward work on the Way.

From 1978 to 1980, however, the Countryside Commission for Scotland and the local authorities took determined steps to bring the route to reality. With help from units of the Regular and Territorial Army, from work parties of the British Trust for Conservation Volunteers, and from Forestry Commission staff, work on bridges, drainage, path cutting and waymarking made steady progress. At Balmaha on 6 October 1980 the West Highland Way was officially opened by Lord Mansfield, then Minister of State at the Scottish Office.

The route has been deservedly popular from the start, and remains so in its third decade of life. Part of it now runs through Scotland's first National Park. The walking surface, infrastructure, interpretation and supporting literature have all been greatly improved, but the experience of walking the Way remains as it always has been, a classic backpacking excursion through some of the finest scenery in Scotland. Try it for yourself: you will not be disappointed.

The Way near Carbeth.

Milngavie – Drymen

SUMMARY

Distance: 19.5km (12 miles).

Height Range: 80-140m.

Terrain: A relatively simple start to the Way on footpaths, tracks, lanes and an old railway with no major climbs. Route accessible by car at numerous points. An easy day's walk.

Lennox

FROM its beginning in Milngavie, north-west of Glasgow, to Inverarnan at the head of Loch Lomond, the West Highland Way runs through the ancient province and earldom of Lennox. Though the name has now largely passed from use, Lennox formerly included all the country between the Campsie Fells in the east and Loch Long in the west, and between the River Clyde and the foot of Glen Falloch. For the purposes of the guide, the long stretch of the Way along the shore of Loch Lomond, which is such a major element of the route, has a chapter to itself. The Lennox chapter therefore takes the way over the ridge north of Milngavie, through Strath Blane and Strath Endrick, and by the forest of Garadhban and the hills of the Highland edge to Loch Lomond. This is the main Lowland part of the West Highland Way, a gentle country of farmland and woodland.

The name Lennox is generally taken to be a Latinised corruption of 'Levenachen', meaning a place of elm trees. It comes from the same root as Leven, which was the old name for Loch Lomond and is still the name of the river by which the loch drains to the Clyde.

The name of Lennox is a thread that runs throughout the fabric of Scottish history. The earliest origins of the lords of Lennox are obscure but the Earldom of Lennox was conferred upon a certain Alwyn Marcarkyl by Malcolm IV when he succeeded to the throne of Scotland in 1153. The Lennox family soon became a force to be reckoned with in feudal Scotland; the fifth Earl, Malcolm, was a staunch supporter of Robert the Bruce during the Wars of Independence, and a signatory to the Declaration of Arbroath.

By the end of the 14th century the Earls had achieved the fullest extent of their land-holding and influence, in a country torn by strife between rival nobles. They then brought about their own downfall by a marriage link with the powerful Dukes of Albany, the nominal Governors of Scotland during the long captivity in England of James l; for on James' return, he made a strong show of his royal authority by summarily executing Albany and the aged Earl Duncan of Lennox at Stirling in 1425. These events provided John Galt with the framework for his historical novel *The Spaewife*.

The unfortunate Earl Duncan left no male heirs. After half a century of internal wrangling over the succession, the earldom of Lennox was arrogated by the Darnley Stewarts in 1488. This family, as close relatives of the Stewart kings, played an important role in every tempestuous reign until the Union of the Crowns in 1603, achieving a short-lived zenith of power in the 18 months marriage of Henry, Lord Darnley, to Mary Queen of Scots, before he was murdered.

The direct line of descent died out in 1672 when the title and lands of Lennox fell to Charles II, who promptly conferred them, with the Dukedom of Richmond, upon an illegitimate son. In 1702 he in turn sold the estates to the Marquis of Montrose, whose family, the Grahams, had held lands in Lennox - mainly at Mugdock and Carbeth - since the 13th century. The Dukes of Montrose thus became the most substantial landowners in Lennox, and retained that distinction until after the First World War.

Milngavie — Carbeth

(7 km; 4.25 miles)

THE West Highland Way begins with an appealing directness. Its start lies less than 10 km from the heart of Scotland's largest city, at a commuter railway station close by a bustling shopping centre; but within a few hundred metres the walker passes out of the urban environment into countryside which rapidly opens out as the Way heads north. As the sardonic old saw puts it, 'Glasgow is a good place to get out of' - the city is close-ringed by fine hill and moorland country. With this rural hinterland, Glasgow has always had a strong outdoor tradition, and Milngavie has long been one of the most popular starting points for outings to the countryside. On summer Sundays in the 1930s, for instance, six times as many trams as on weekdays ran to the Milngavie terminus. It is, then, very appropriate that the West Highland Way, which in its early evolution was fostered by the Glasgow outdoor fraternity, should begin its northward course at Milngavie.

Assuming that you are starting from Glasgow city centre, you have an ample choice of transport to the start of the Way. The Trans-Clyde electric train service operates

regular services from the main line termini at Queen Street or Central Stations, though it may be necessary to change at Partick. There is a frequent bus service to Milngavie from the bus station at the north end of Buchanan Street. It is also perfectly possible to walk out to Milngavie, using the Clyde and Kelvin Walkways — see page vii and viii for details.

When asking directions or buying tickets, visitors can avoid confusion and perhaps some amusement at their expense by remembering that Milngavie is pronounced approximately 'Mull-guy'. It has been suggested that the name derives from the Gaelic *Muileann-gaoithe*, meaning a windmill. The etymology seems rather doubtful but in any event the name appears on 17th century maps as Milguy, and its anglicisation appears to be relatively recent. The down-to-earth Glaswegian humour ascribes it to Milngavie's rather 'upper-crust' image — the town is now a large commuter suburb of Glasgow. A wit of the 1920s declared:

'Yet I have heard that in Milngavie,
The folk are quite reserved and shy,
And every house has got a slavey,
Who's taught to call the place Milngavie.'

As late as the 1790s, however, Milngavie was a tiny village of about 200 inhabitants, owing its livelihood to the Allander Water which supplied the power for several mills, including a snuffmill and a paper mill, as well as water for the bleaching of textiles. In common with many other towns in the West of Scotland, Milngavie grew with the cotton industry, and by 1835 its population had increased six-fold. The southern approaches to the town pass some of the riverside meadows in which bleaching fabrics were watered and exposed to the sun, though no trace of the industry now remains. From the same vicinity the Campsie Fells appear invitingly close over the low ridge between Milngavie and Strath Blane to the north.

As well as the railway station, there are bus stops and ample car-parking facilities nearby. From the station a pedestrian underpass leads under Woodburn Way and up a flight of steps into Station Road, which after about 150 metres continues into Douglas Street. This pedestrian

Opposite: Mugdock Loch.

precinct offers a wide range of shops, banks, cafes and restaurants. Since there is no comparable shopping centre on the Way before Fort William, at the other end, you might like to take the opportunity to top up on any supplies you need here.

The Way leaves Douglas Street at the bridge over the Allander Water. Just past a granite monolith unveiled in 1992, marking the official start point, it runs down a walkway ramp over the stream, northwards around a small car-park at the rear of the shops, across a road and along a tarmac path for 100 metres or so. It then passes under another road to enter a sunken, tree-lined lane on the line of an old railway that served a former paper mill on the Allander Water. As this lane heads north, the noise and bustle of the town rapidly recede.

Shortly after it passes the Milngavie Community Education Centre on the left, the Way leaves the former railway, turning left and right to the Allander Water. It follows the east bank of the stream through pleasant, wooded parkland for 400 metres or so before striking rightwards and uphill away from the riverbank, climbing gradually to the upper part of Allander Park, a rough moorland of birch, broom and gorse above the town.

From near the crest of this rise there is a pleasant view southwards over the suburban fringes of Glasgow, and westwards along the front of the Kilpatrick hills. The ridge on which you now stand, and which the Way crosses as it heads north, is part of the same geological formation as the Kilpatricks and the Campsie Fells, although they are a good deal higher. All were formed by great lava flows in the Lower Carboniferous period, some 350 million years ago, which may originally have covered as much as 1500 square km (600 sq. miles) and have been well over 600 metres (2000 feet) thick. Despite having been much eroded and faulted over time, these Clyde Plateau Lavas still appear as upstanding hill masses in the Central 'Lowlands' of Scotland. A conspicuous feature of the formation is the 'tiered' effect created by successive lava flows, which is well seen in the face of the Campsies above Strath Blane, and in looking back to the Kilpatricks from the Drymen area.

The Way now turns left (north-eastwards) over an open moor of bracken and birch to follow a long ride, the former drive to Craigallian House, through Mugdock Wood. Mugdock is a long-established mixed wood notable for its flowers and insect population. Here in spring and summer you will find many of the small grassland flowers that grow along much of the length of the West Highland Way. One of the brightest and most prolific is the little yellow tormentil, but others, so common that even non-botanists will quickly come to recognise them, include the heath bedstraw, with clusters of tiny white flowers, and the delicate blue milkwort. In ditches and damper places the pink lousewort and the purplish pom-pom of the scabious are common. There, too, you will find the butterwort, a violet flower hanging gracefully on a tall stem that rises from a flat rosette of yellow-green leaves. The leaves curl up to catch and digest small insects. Where the ground is very wet the sundew takes over the insectivorous role, with round red leaf-pads covered in sticky hairs to entrap flies.

In 1980 Mugdock Wood, together with land to the north-east, around the ancient ruin of Mugdock Castle, was gifted by Sir Hugh Fraser to provide a country park for the people of Glasgow. The park is run by the Mugdock Management Committee on behalf of East Dumbartonshire and Stirling Councils — the boundary between council areas follows the southern edge of Mugdock Wood and the Allander Water. It includes an area of oak woodland (a Site of Special Scientific Interest), the ruins of two castles and an attractive loch. Public facilities include a visitor centre, several car parks, picnic sites and a network of footpaths and bridleways. The park has its own website at *www.mugdock-country-park.org.uk*.

At the end of the old drive through the wood, the Way turns leftwards down a minor road for a few metres, then resumes its course turning right through a stile onto a track winding along the rushy flats by the Allander burn and up the west shore of Craigallian Loch. On this stretch you will have your first view of Dumgoyne, the hunchback, knobbly hill at the western end of the Campsies, which dominates the Way through Strath Blane and remains visible far to the north. The West Highland Way is favoured with a succession of these 'mountain mileposts', hills of distinctive character by which you can measure progress, and which change their aspect as you pass. Dumgoyne is the first of them, and one of the finest despite its modest height of 427 metres (1402 feet).

Craigallian Loch, overlooked by the turreted Victorian mansion of Craigallian House, lies in a shallow scoop through the ridge between Milngavie and Strath Blane, a scoop probably cut by an over-riding arm of the great glacier that flowed southwards through Strath Blane from the Highland icefields during the last glaciation. The rough, wooded hill-slopes around the loch have been well-known as a weekend escape for generations of Glaswegians, from the Victorian and Edwardian naturalists to the thousands of Boy Scouts who have over the years come to the nearby camp at Auchengillan.

It was, however, during the Depression that Craigallian achieved its apotheosis, in 'The Fire' - a bonfire on the slopes above the loch where weekenders and unemployed made their rendezvous, ate, gossiped, and sang. There are many stirring tales of the tough characters and rough living of those days: of men who, unable to afford sleeping-bags, slept in brown paper or under the *Glasgow Herald* - which they preferred to lesser newspapers not for the quality of its journalism but for the size of its pages; of fights on wet dark nights for the restricted comforts of a telephone kiosk; of epic journeys by lorry or motor-bike to tackle desperate climbs with primitive equipment. For these folk there will always be a certain magic in the Craigallian area, where later comers see only the spruce plantation above the loch.

There is further evidence of the escape to the country in the little holiday huts around the Way where it goes down to the right beyond the gate at the plantation's edge. These are only a fraction of the numbers of huts scattered around the hill to the west, on the Carbeth estate; all were built before or shortly after the War, when planning regulations were less stringent than they are now, and it is a tribute to the loving care and effort devoted to their maintenance that so many still remain.

The Way crosses the outflow from Carbeth Loch, then goes up to join an estate driveway a short distance before it meets the B821 road at a gateway which rejoices in the name of Ballachalairy Yett - 'yett' being an old Scots word for 'gate'. This section of the Way can be ended here, by going east along the B821 and down the steep zig-zag of Cuilt Brae to Blanefield, which offers shopping facilities, accommodation, and bus services back to Glasgow; or by going 1.5 km (about a mile) westwards to the A809 Stockiemuir Road and the Glasgow-Drymen bus service. The Way goes westwards, but only for some 300 metres to where a stile on the right leads into the 'Tinker's Loan', a broad ride between parallel stone dykes, rising with an attractive air of expectancy to a stile on the skyline, with the Campsie Fells beyond it. The name and appearance of this ride indicate that it is an old roadway, probably dating back to the days before enclosure of the fields.

The crest at the head of the Loan, though unspectacular in itself, marks an important early stage in the Way. It is the edge of the Glasgow basin or 'howe', the watershed from which the streams drain northwards and westwards into Loch Lomond, and from which the Way descends again to only a few metres above sea-level. In clear weather this - or perhaps a point a little further down to the north - is one of the Way's finer viewpoints, the wide vista to the north being enclosed by the Kilpatricks on the one hand and the rugged scarp of the Campsies on the other. The immediate foreground is rather rough, but is offset by the steep wooded knoll of Dumgoyach and the fertile chequerboard of the Lennox plains, with the Highland edge beyond. In good visibility the horizon shows a long frieze of mountains, from Ben Ledi on the right, round to the far Crianlarich hills, but your eye will probably settle on the broad-shouldered bulk of Ben Lomond, towards the left, another mountain milepost marking the first quarter of the distance to Fort William. You are now well started on the Way.

Carbeth — Drymen

(12.5 km; 7.75 miles)

Please note that dogs must be kept on leads on this section.

THE stretch of the Way from the ridgecrest at Carbeth to the A811 road near Drymen is the most pleasantly domestic part of the whole route, and passes through its richest farmland. As you descend into Strath Blane, you may well feel inclined to agree with the author of the Old Statistical Account at the end of the 18th century, who suggested that the visitor would here be charmed with 'the verdure of the country, the mildness of the air, and the appearance of cheerfulness and plenty, which is displayed around... In summer, the landscape is enriched and adorned by the luxuriant foliage of the woods with which the hills are skirted...'

There are also hereabouts the signs of a long continuity of human occupation. The cottages of Arlehaven, which the Way skirts before it turns leftwards towards Dumgoyach, are relatively modern; but the lands of 'Erleleven', as part of the estates of Duntreath, were granted by King James I to his brother-in-law William Edmonstone around 1434, after the King had broken the power of the Earls of Lennox. The grant was confirmed in 1452 by James II, who further erected the estate into the Barony of Duntreath. The 'reddendo' or token rental for these lands, to be produced on demand at Duntreath 'at the feast of the nativity of John the Baptist', was one pound of pepper; and the lands are still held by the Edmonstone family.

Again, as the Way descends over what used to be rather boggy ground on the slopes below Arlehaven — where you may find among the rushes such fine marsh flowers as the austere white grass of Parnassus — it passes, on the ridge to your right, the Dumgoyach Standing Stones. These five large boulders aligned roughly north-west to south-east are thought to date back to Neolithic times, when the open ground above Strath Blane may have offered easier cultivation than the valley floor, which would probably have been ill-drained and densely wooded. Radio-carbon dating of charcoal found there during an excavation in 1972 suggested a date around 3500BC. The Stones have limited interest for close examination, and you can best contribute to their conservation by viewing them from a distance.

The remarkably steep, wooded cone of Dumgoyach, which the Way turns on its west flank, is one of the remnant volcanoes from which the Clyde Plateau lavas emerged — that is, the resistant neck through which the lavas flowed upwards and outwards in successive layers. Dumgoyach is almost pure basalt, while other similar necks like Dumgoyne and Dumfoyne, the less distinctive bump to the south-east of Dumgoyne, contain basalt agglomerates: they show remaining fragments of the rock through which the volcanic vent pushed its way. The Campsies present a fine steep rampart above Strath Blane, and can be approached by several routes from the valley. The basalt crags on the hill fronts should be avoided, for the rock is as a rule extremely friable and loose.

Close under Dumgoyach, the Way goes round the west side of Dumgoyach Farm, down a lane and along the farm road to cross the Blane Water by a plank bridge. Just beyond the bridge, it turns left on to the old track of the Blane Valley railway line, which it follows for the next 6.5 km (4 miles) to near Gartness. As might be expected, the former railway line gives pleasant and easy walking, especially in dry conditions: after rain it can be rather muddy. It is crossed by a substantial number of farm access lanes, and a succession of metal V-stiles at each will slow you somewhat.

The Blane Valley Railway was opened to passengers in 1867, as far as Killearn Station — later Dumgoyne Station— where the Way now crosses the A81 road for the first time; in 1882 it was extended northwards to Aberfoyle. The promoters had hoped that Glasgow's wealthier businessmen would build their houses in Strath Blane and commute to the city by railway, but the line was a circuitous one and traffic was always light. Not surprisingly the line was one of the early casualties of post-war rationalisation of the railways. Passenger services were withdrawn in 1951, and the line closed completely in 1959.

However, even before its adoption for the West Highland Way the old Blane Valley line had taken on a new lease of life as a routeway for the 1520 mm (60 inch) water pipeline which is used by East of Scotland Water to transport water from Loch Lomond to consumers throughout Central Scotland, including some as far away as Livingston in West Lothian. It is this buried pipeline that forms the raised embankment along the old railway track. This convenient route in the valley bottom contrasts with the line taken by the much older pipeline that carries Glasgow's water supply from its

Overleaf: Craigallian Loch

main source at Loch Katrine in the Trossachs: it runs along the hillside some way above the A81.

In fact the great flat-bottomed trench of Strath Blane provides an excellent natural routeway through the hill ranges on either side. The valley is the product of a variety of geological factors and is clearly not the result of erosion by the relatively small Blane Water. It is partly a fault-controlled valley, the southern fault being represented in the steep brae below Arlehaven; geologists argue that it may be a remnant of an ancient river system that once drained south-eastwards towards the Forth estuary.

Certainly the strath was further eroded by ice during the Pleistocene glaciation, and it has been suggested that the valley's flat floor represents the sandy bed of a lake trapped by an ice-sheet that blocked the northwards drainage as the Highland ice retreated. As evidence of the character of the valley floor, you will notice not only the fertility of its soil, but also the absence of dykes as field boundaries, due to the lack of boulders or rock outcrops.

As the Way continues under the craggy shoulders of Dumgoyne, it passes on the right the distillery and bond warehouses of Glen Goyne, which has been producing malt whisky, mainly for blending, for nearly a century and a half. It was formerly known as Glenguin, a name which has passed into the peerage, for that was the title taken by Lord Tedder, Marshal of the Royal Air Force, who was born in one of the houses uphill from the distillery in 1890. Tedder achieved great success in partnerships with Generals Auchinleck and Alexander in the Western Desert campaigns of World War Two before going on to act as Deputy Supreme Commander in Europe to General Eisenhower from 1943 to 1945; he died in 1967.

The distillery is open to visitors, and a notice on the Way indicates a path across to it, and extends an invitation to sample 'Scotland's unpeated malt whisky'. It is open all year, with regular conducted tours (afternoons only on Sundays). The diversion to see how whisky is produced is well worth while if you have the time.

Two other famous men are associated with the Strath Blane area, or more precisely with the parish of Killearn, which lies between this point and the River Endrick. George Buchanan and John Napier both made major contributions to the European Renaissance, though in very different fields. Napier is now the better known of the two, for his work was largely in mathematics, and he is credited with the invention of logarithms. He lived at various times at Gartness Castle, which stood by the Endrick some way further north. Buchanan, scholar, philosopher and poet, tutor to James VI of Scotland and I of England, was born at the humble farmstead of Moss, which may be seen half-hidden in trees south-west of the Way a few hundred metres after it crosses the busy A81 at the former Dumgoyne station.

The original house is long gone, but at the road crossing is the Beech Tree Inn, which offers food and drink all day and has picnic tables outside.

George Buchanan (1506-82) lived in troubled times, both in Scotland during the hectic reign of Mary Queen of Scots, and in Europe, where he travelled widely, as the Reformation ran its course. As Professor Christopher Smout has pointed out, it is ironic that Buchanan's huge contemporary reputation, based on his mastery of Latin, the *lingua franca* of the Renaissance, has dwindled away almost to vanishing point as the study of Latin has declined, while the name of Napier (1550-1617) his near contemporary, has grown with mathematics. However, George Buchanan was not forgotten by his countrymen, who erected a large obelisk to his memory in Killearn village. You can catch a glimpse of this monument through the trees around the village from higher points a little further north along the Way.

In this vicinity the Way goes through a rather semi-urban phase, as it passes successively a small factory making conservatories, the Killearn sewage plant, and a garage, while it parallels the main road. A little further on, on the west side of the road, is the site of Killearn Hospital, covering around 20 hectares. The hospital was built prior to the Second World War as an emergency unit to treat the expected casualties of bombing raids on the Glasgow conurbation, and for nearly 30 years after the war it served as a specialist neuro-surgical unit before closing in 1972. Most of the site has now been cleared.

Close beyond the hospital the Way passes under the B834, which incidentally leads eastwards within 1.5 km to Killearn, a quiet village given a new lease of life in recent

years by an influx of Glasgow commuters, and offering a
range of shops and some accommodation. There is now
a clear sense of having moved into a new province, out
of the narrower views of Strath Blane, a sense confirmed
as the old railway rises gradually to cross the A81 road
for the second time. This higher ground offers wide prospects east along the northern front of the Campsies, west
across the open farmland of Strath Endrick, and north to
the Highland edge. As if in confirmation of the change
of scene, the topography also changes, swelling in soft
rolling ridges that stretch from here on to Drymen. These
are the remains of a great sheet of sand and gravel laid
down at the front of an ice-lobe which flowed down the
valley of Loch Lomond to sprawl outwards across the
piedmont plain of Lennox in the final readvance of the
last glaciation, only some 12,000 years ago. Conic Hill is
visible, and in clear conditions the summit of Ben Lomond
can be seen.

About 750 metres after crossing the A81 road, the Way
finally leaves the old Blane Valley railway. It climbs up
by the bridge and turns west on the minor road from
Killearn to Drymen a short distance from Gartness. This
is a pleasant, rambling country lane, but you should be
wary of traffic, particularly at bends and on narrower
sections.

From the railway the road dips gently down to cross
the River Endrick by the douce hamlet of Gartness, a little
terrace of cottages facing the river with no two houses
quite alike. The starkly functional modern bridge of 1971
replaced an old one dating from 1715; in the autumn it
provides an excellent platform from which to view
salmon leaping up the rapids on their way to spawning
grounds in the headwaters of the Endrick. At this point the
Way enters the Loch Lomond and the Trossachs National
Park.

Beneath the bridge the river courses over great slabby
ledges, the beds of the Old Red Sandstone. These rocks
of Devonian age floor the wide valley between the Highland edge and the volcanic plateaux of the Campsies and
the Kilpatricks. As the Gartness cottages show, the sandstone makes a pleasant, warm building stone.

The old mill lade under the bridge hints at past activity. A few hundred metres down-river there are ruins of

other mills; one of them incorporates stones from the medieval Gartness Castle, which once stood nearby, though nothing of it now remains. The lands of Gartness passed into the hands of the Napier family, who also held the estate of Merchiston, near Edinburgh, during the 15th-century squabbles over the Earldom of Lennox, to which the Napiers, like the Darnley Stewarts, had a claim by marriage.

It was at Gartness Castle that John Napier, the philosopher and mathematician, is said to have stayed on occasion. According to tradition he had many of the attributes of an absentminded professor; he would order the watermill by the Castle to be shut off temporarily when its creaking machinery disturbed his studies, and he was inclined to wander about the Endrick banks at night in his nightgown and cap, lost in thought. Not surprisingly, the local folk were firmly of the opinion that he was a warlock in league with the Devil.

Following the road, the Way climbs westward over another old railway line to the top of the ridge by Upper Gartness Farm. This was the Forth and Clyde Junction Railway, opened in 1856 to link Stirling and the Vale of Leven, in the hope of competing successfully with the major east-west lines south of the Campsies; but like the Blane Valley line, which joined it a little to the east, the Forth and Clyde Junction was never much more than a useful farmers' line with some seasonal tourist traffic. This section was closed to passengers as long ago as 1934 and is now a rich, tangled corridor of birchwood, gorse and bramble and a happy hunting ground for the naturalist.

The top of the hill by Upper Gartness gives an excellent panorama over the fertile farmland of Strath Endrick, with the river winding against high banks cut into the fluvio-glacial deposits. The north face of the Campsie Fells shows a rugged front in which volcanic necks stand out as resistant craggy buttresses separating deep-sculpted corries. Dumgoyach stands sentinel at the head of Strath Blane, and to the west and north the hills around Loch Lomond begin to assert their individuality: the little crag-and-tail of Duncryne above Gartocharn, well-known as the personal viewpoint of Tom Weir, climber, author and naturalist; the shapely Luss Hills above the Loch's west shore; and the knobbly ridge of Conic Hill above

Balmaha, your next milestone. Conic Hill marks the line of the great Highland Boundary Fault that runs from near Helensburgh on the Clyde, to Stonehaven on the east coast, and so divides Highlands from Lowlands, at least in geological terms.

As the Way follows the minor road first westwards and then northwards along the Drumquhassle ridge towards Drymen, the contrast between the rolling patchwork of farmland and hedgerow on either hand, and the moorland and forest to the north becomes more evident. Some 1900 years ago the Romans built a small fort here as part of a chain of frontier posts along the Highland edge. No trace remains above ground level, and though the existence of a fort hereabouts was long suspected — even the corrupt placename Drumquhassle, 'castle ridge', may refer to it — only aerial photography revealed the site. But the proximity of the Highlands to the rich lands of Lennox and Menteith kept the area in a state of constant anxiety well into the 18th century. Its herds of fat cattle and flocks of sheep lay practically at the mercy of raids and incursions from the more lawless Highland clans, of whom the most notorious were the MacGregors living around the heads of Loch Lomond and Loch Katrine.

The depredations inflicted on the hapless Lowland farmers were so regular, and the forces of law and order so impotent against the reivers, that the MacGregors and others were able to transmute their activities from a high-risk enterprise with irregular and unpredictable returns into a rather more secure and formalised fiscal trading arrangement with guaranteed income. In modern terms, they went into a protection racket. In return for payment of blackmail by the landholders most at risk, they guaranteed to prevent the theft of cattle and damage to property by Highland caterans, and to recover or make restitution for losses suffered. Since most of the raids had been conducted by themselves, it was not difficult to stop them: but it does seem that the blackmail contracts were honoured on most occasions, when other malefactors were pursued — sometimes far into the Highlands — and made to give up their spoils.

To modern eyes the legal formality of the surviving contracts, with their attested signatures, penalty clauses, and nicely fixed rates of payment — in one example £4 per year per £100 valuation of a farmer's landholding — has a slightly absurd quality. For the suffering Lowland farmers, however, there was no humour in the situation. They were caught between the Devil and the deep blue sea, for the civil authorities, while practically powerless to control the MacGregors, prohibited any sort of treatying with them and threatened to take stern measures against the signatories of blackmail contracts. For all that, the authorities themselves would on occasion contract with the MacGregors to provide a force, dignified by the title of 'The Watch', to prevent raids and incursions. The famous Rob Roy served in such a 'legal' Watch as a young man.

At Easter Drumquhassle — which also provides B&B — you will find the first of the chain of wooden 'wigwams'

Approaching Conic Hill

provided along the West Highland Way in 1995. These simple shelters are designed by Charles Gulland to use available local timber, making them easy and inexpensive to erect. They offer low-cost accommodation on a sleeping platform; a form of indoor camping, if you like.

From the road on the crest of the ridge there is a glimpse of the lower part of Loch Lomond and some of its wooded islands over the policies of Buchanan Castle, the former residence of the Dukes of Montrose. ('Policies' is a Scottish term for the grounds or parkland of a large

house.) Just along here is an Ordnance Survey triangula-
tion pillar, right beside the road. These pillars were a vital part of the national mapping survey until very recent
times. There are over 5,000 of them in the UK as a whole,
but the vast majority have now been made redundant
through the use of satellites. A considerable number, in
scenic areas and on summits, have been 'adopted' by individuals or groups, who now maintain them. This one,
however, moulders quietly in its field.

The road gradually descends past a large quarry on
the left and the plantation of Gateside on the right; where
it turns westward towards Drymen by the entrance to
Gateside, an old right-of-way path used by generations
of schoolchildren takes the Way northwards across an
open field by a burn and up the brae to the A811 road
immediately east of its junction with the B858 to Drymen,
and opposite the Drymen Primary School and school-
house. These buildings, like those at Gartness, use the
warm red local sandstone. You have now entered the
National Park.

The Way here turns eastwards for a short distance along
the main road. However, on either the B858 or the minor
road at Gateside it is less than a kilometre westwards to
Drymen. This pleasant village centres round a small
green, an unusual feature in Scottish rural settlements.
As 'Drumyn', from the Gaelic, 'a little ridge', it is first
mentioned in a charter of 1238 in which Alwyn, Earl of
Lennox, granted lands to Paisley Abbey. It is now a route
centre from which bus services run to Glasgow, Stirling,
Aberfoyle, Balloch at the foot of Loch Lomond, and to
Balmaha, where the Way reaches the loch. Walkers wishing to take the low road for reasons of weather or lack of
fitness can rejoin the West Highland Way at Balmaha, or
in the Garadhban woods north of Drymen by taking the
minor road to Gartmore which runs up from the head of
the green.

Drymen offers not only hotel and bed-and-breakfast
accommodation, but also a range of shops and services
not matched along the Way till Kinlochleven, nearly 100
km further north. In particular, the village boasts the last
bank to be found in all that distance. Like the travellers
of old, Waywalkers will do well to look to their purses
before crossing the Highland Line.

On Craigie Fort.

Drymen – Rowardennan

SUMMARY

Distance: 22.5km (14 miles).

Height Range: 20-358m.

Terrain: Good paths or tracks most of the way. The first major climb is over Conic Hill (358m) near Balmaha. The lochside route to Rowardennan is twisty and surprisingly undulating, with intermittent good views as you wind through the woods.

Please note that dogs are not allowed on Conic Hill even on a lead.

Drymen—Balmaha

(10.5 km; 6.5 miles)

FROM Drymen school the A811 runs eastwards in a purposeful line that contrasts with the ambling farm roads the Way has followed from Gartness. Even if the map did not make it explicit, the straightness of the road over hill and dip would suggest its origins as an old military road, built soon after the Jacobite Rising of 1745 to link the castles at Stirling and Dumbarton.

As you begin the 10 km (6 mile) stretch to Balmaha, you can be excused for feeling that you are making it hard for yourself as the next milepost, Conic Hill, recedes behind your left shoulder. However, after about 400 metres along the main road, the Way strikes north opposite the steading of Blarnavaid farm and climbs steadily by farm and forest track before beginning a long westwards traverse through the Garadhban Forest at around 150 metres (500 feet).

The Forestry Commission's holdings of over 500 hectares (1300 acres) at Garadhban date back to 1931, so there is some well established old timber in the plantations. However, Garadhban suffered severely in the great West of Scotland gale of January 1968, which caused widespread damage to property and woodland. There has been some benefit, in that the long process of clearing the windthrown timber, followed by replanting, has increased the ecological variety of the forest and created a variety of age-classes in the plantations. As a result these woods are particularly interesting for ornithologists, who may have the luck to see less common bird species such as crossbill or siskin. Even the casual observer walking quietly through may encounter a capercaillie, the largest of British game birds; the cock bird, like a dark-coloured turkey, is usually first heard then seen, as it thrashes noisily away through the trees.

The windthrow and recent planting also provide windows through the woods, giving excellent wide views back over the lowlands. As the Way crosses the minor road to Gartmore and turns west, the main features of interest gradually change, from the Campsies through the Buchanan Castle estates to the Endrick marshes and Loch Lomond.

The high quality rural landscape of these lowlands, in which farmland and woodland intermingle to fine effect, owes much to the activity of successive Dukes of Montrose. At the end of the 17th century the third Marquis of Montrose purchased the estates of Buchanan from the creditors of the last Buchanan laird, and a little later his son, the first Duke, added the substantial remaining estates of Lennox. The family thus came to control the whole east shore of Loch Lomond.

The third Duke of Montrose (1755-1836) was a particularly energetic 'improver'; in the New Statistical Account the parish minister described him as 'an able persevering patron of agriculture. During a long life he was unwearied in embellishing his residence at Buchanan, in improving and extending his plantations, and in introducing superior breeds of farm stock.'

The superbly wooded parklands to the west of Drymen were planted to complement the vast baronial mansion of Buchanan Castle, built between 1854 and 1857 to replace an earlier house destroyed by fire. During the Second World War it served as a military hospital, but thereafter it lay empty and was partly demolished. A large part of the Montrose estates was sold after the death of the fifth Duke in 1925, but much of the finest woodland was preserved, particularly within the Queen Elizabeth Forest Park on Loch Lomondside.

At the end of the long traverse the excellent forest roads run out first into a grassy track through young Norway spruce, and then into a well-surfaced path through an old plantation. From this woodland tunnel the Way emerges over a stile into rough, bracken-clad moorland pasture, stretching over to the barrier hills of the Highland edge, which seem suddenly close at hand. Leftwards the moor slopes down into farmland and woodland above the levels of Loch Lomond. The contrast with the sheltered enclosure of the Garadhban is sharply invigorating.

The next stretch, at one time difficult to follow in midsummer, when the bracken may reach over head-height in places, is now a fine machine path. Over the moor to the northwest, you keep the dyke on your right as far as the bridge over the sonorously named Kilandan Blandan burn - incidentally the first of the purpose-built Way bridges you have met. Thereafter, bear left to the bridge over the Burn of Mar, which occupies a delightful site deep-set among rowan and birch: an idyllic lunch-spot for a warm day, especially with the 200 metre (700 feet) climb over Conic Hill in prospect. This little burn, like others along the Way, is the haunt of warblers, dippers and wrens.

At the top of the steep little rib above the bridge, the slope of Conic Hill rises beyond. The Way breaks off to rise steadily across the heathery banks of the hill. The gradual ascent, looking out over the bare moorland drained by the Burn of Mar, ends where the Way turns on to the north-west side of Conic Hill, to traverse its north face on a natural bench beneath the humpback ridgecrest.

From this traverse splendid views open up to the north-west, but it is well worthwhile to climb up to the top of Conic - start from the point where the Way begins to drop westwards - to enjoy one of the widest and most varied panoramas of the whole West Highland Way.

The hill itself is a fairly steep-sided hogsback ridge. It does appear conical from end-on, particularly from near Balmaha, but its name is less likely to come from its shape than from the Gaelic *A'Coinneach,* the moss or bog, which may be a transference from the moorland on its north and east. Conic Hill owes its distinctive character to the Highland Boundary Fault, and the trend of the fault is very obvious in the alignment of the islands in Loch Lomond.

But geology is rarely as simple as it seems: Conic is not a Highland rock formation raised by faulting above the Lowlands, but the resistant edges of Lowland strata, warped to a high angle by the fault-line, which is actually to the north of the ridge. At several places on the top of the hill you can examine this rock, a chunky conglomerate of lower Old Red Sandstone age. It is full of varied and

The Luss Hills from Conic Hill.

interesting fragments of older rocks, ranging in size from pebbles to boulders, cemented together by a dark red or almost purple sandstone; and on the descent towards Balmaha, you can readily observe, on looking back, how steeply inclined the beds of sandstone lie. On or close to the ridge-top there are also one or two foreign-looking erratic boulders of quite different formation, left behind by glacier ice as it overrode the ridge.

While much of the panorama from Conic Hill is a grander version of the southwards view from near Gartness or Garadhban, the added height gives it a new dimension. To the east, Ben Ledi near Callander appears as a flattened pyramid left of Gualann; to Gualann's right the distant Ochil plateau presents an abrupt scarp to the south, where in good visibility the Wallace Monument on Abbey Craig can be seen in the Stirling gap. The Gargunnock and Fintry Hills lead round to the familiar north front of the Campsies and to Strath Blane, beyond which you may spy the tops of some of the tower block flats of Glasgow. On the Kilpatrick hills the bun-shaped top of Duncolm, the highest point, is another old volcanic vent; to its right, through the gap of the Vale of Leven, the chimney of the Inverkip power station marks the Clyde. Beyond it the mountains of the Isle of Arran are a bonus in clear weather.

In the foreground the Endrick meanders reluctantly into Loch Lomond. The marshes at its mouth, part of the Loch Lomond National Nature Reserve, are famous among bird-watchers for wildfowl and waders. But the *piece de resistance* of the Conic view is Loch Lomond itself, which here for the first time presents its true character as a loch of both Highlands and Lowlands. Sir Walter Scott epitomised this aspect in *Rob Roy:*

> '. . . this noble lake, boasting innumerable beautiful islands of every varying form and outline which fancy can frame - its northern extremity narrowing until it is lost among dusky and retreating mountains - while, gradually widening as it extends to the southward, it spreads its base around the indentures and promontories of a fair and fertile land, offers one of the most surprising, beautiful, and sublime spectacles in nature.'

Overleaf: A busy scene at Balmaha.

On a clear day, the Way walker will enjoy a most inviting prospect of the route ahead, passing from sight where Ben Lomond looks over the loch to the rugged peaks of the Arrochar Alps. From there onwards, the West Highland Way is continuously in mountain country.

The easiest descent from the top of Conic Hill is to retrace your steps to the Way and continue the westwards traverse. The route drops steeply into a little grassy corrie between two limbs of the ridge, then turns down through a gap to the south-east, descending a built-up staircase on steep slopes which in summer are covered in deep bracken. At its foot a track leads westwards again under the hillslope to the forest edge, and down through mature plantations to join a forest walk which emerges at the public car park in Balmaha. The Way crosses the car park, and comes out on to the B837 road at the head of Balmaha bay. In the winter months Balmaha is a quiet backwater, but in summer the road and car park are thronged, the pavements crowded, and the bay choked with a colourful multitude of small boats.

Although it is a small settlement, Balmaha is an old-established one. It appears as 'Balmacha' in Blaeu's Atlas of the mid 17th century, and may be much older, since it is thought to owe its name to St Maha or Mahew, a companion of St Patrick, who may have been a missionary in this area. Near the farm of Moorpark, above the Garadhban woods, there is a St Maha's Well which was long reputed by local people to have healing powers.

Under the active promotion of woodland management by the Dukes of Montrose, Balmaha became the site of a small factory producing pyrolignous acid or 'wood vinegar', a crude acetic acid, by distillation from oak thinnings and trimmings. The acid was used in the textile bleaching and dyeing industry in the Vale of Leven and the Glasgow area. At its peak the factory used up to 700 tonnes of small wood each year, but it closed during the 1920s when large-scale industrial production of chemicals took over the market.

Today the main activity in Balmaha is catering for day visitors; there is a shop and tearoom, a visitor centre, pub and bed and breakfast accommodation. A limited bus service runs south via Drymen to Balloch and the Vale of Leven, but there is no scheduled bus service north to Rowardennan.

Boat trips on the loch and to the islands are available, and if you have time to spare, a visit to Inchcailloch, the nearest of the islands, is recommended. Inchcailloch is part of the Loch Lomond National Nature Reserve and has an excellent nature trail which describes the geology and the natural and human history of the island.

During the 1930s boats were among the many means by which outdoor enthusiasts contrived to squeeze a full day on the hills from a one-day weekend. Jock Nimlin, one of the most enterprising climbers of the time, has described how he and his companions would catch a late bus from Glasgow on a Saturday night to arrive at Balmaha about midnight: 'sometimes we arranged for a rowing-boat to be ready at Balmaha jetty and, rowing with two pairs of oars in two-hour shifts, we would cover the 14 miles to Tarbet by 4am, snatch a few hours' sleep under the trees and walk to Arrochar for a fair day's climbing before facing the return trip… I can still recall the bliss of an off-shift when one curled up between the feet of the swinging oarsmen — took a last look at the swaying stars and drifted into sleep to the slap and gurgle of the water.'

Loch Lomond

LOCH Lomond is the largest body of inland water in Britain, covering over 70 square kilometres (27 square miles). It is one of the longest Scottish lochs, at 37 km (23 miles) and one of the deepest: south of Inversnaid the bed of the loch drops to a depth of 190 metres (623 feet), of which all but 8 metres (27 feet) lies below sea-level. By general consent it is also among the most beautiful of Scottish lochs. In July 2002, the Loch Lomond and Trossachs area was officially designated Scotland's first National Park, an accolade it fully deserves. This should bring an injection of extra money for the conservation of the area and enable genuinely co-ordinated management of recreation, agriculture, water use and economic activity, to the benefit of the area as a whole. The West Highland Way follows the eastern shore of the loch for about 30 km (19 miles), giving the walker a vivid appreciation of its changing character and noble scenery.

The accepted view of geomorphologists is that Loch Lomond probably did not exist prior to the Pleistocene glaciation. Its site was occupied by the high headwaters of three rivers flowing east, with the divides between them roughly on the lines: Ben Vorlich-Beinn a'Choin and Ben Reoch-Ben Lomond. During the Ice Age these watersheds were breached by one of the great glaciers radiating from the vast zone of ice accumulation on Rannoch Moor, and a deep north-south trench was excavated.

As a result of these processes, Loch Lomond is in two distinct sections. In its southern part, up to Ross Point, the loch is wide, relatively shallow, and studded with islands. North from Ross Point it is rarely more than 1500 metres (a mile) wide, is enclosed between steeply sloping hillsides that continue down to great depths, and has only a few small islands. It is a loch of both Highland and Lowland, a contrast reflected in climate, vegetation, wildlife and human history. The relatively flat low ground of the southern end, with moderate rainfall, is good arable farmland. It gradually gives way northwards to pasture and woodland, including Scotland's largest remnant of oakwood, on the slopes above the loch, which in turn pass upwards and northwards into bare open moorland and mountain characterised by high rainfall, extreme exposure and thin soils.

The area surrounding the loch presents a remarkable botanical variety: a quarter of all known British flowering plants and ferns have been found in the Loch Lomond catchment. Similarly the gamut from marshland to mountain-top habitats attracts a wide variety of bird species, further augmented by the loch's position at a crossroads of migration routes; some 220 species have been observed. There is a correspondingly wide range of mammals, from shrews to red deer, fallow deer and feral goats, and even a notable diversity of types of fish. The loch holds not only the common Scottish game fish, salmon, sea-trout and brown trout, and a number of coarse fish such as perch and roach (and some monster pike), but also a curiosity called the powan (*Coregonus*). This fresh-water herring, found in only a few other locations in Britain, was probably isolated in Loch Lomond during sea-level changes after the last glaciation, and may now be the most common fish in the loch.

In terms of human history the Loch Lomond area has been both a corridor of movement and a zone of conflict. While the people of the low country at the foot of the loch were settled farmers on land rented from titled magnates, those inhabiting the rough terrain to the north were small clans of lawless cattle traders and reivers; the interaction of the two kept the region in a state of tension for centuries. Into the 19th century a considerable population occupied the shores of even the Highland section of the loch; but most of the people and settlements have gone, and it is now difficult even to envisage the clachans that are listed in contemporary accounts at frequent intervals along the loch shore.

As a result of its accessibility from the Lowlands, Loch Lomond attracted many early travellers who were particularly intrigued by persistent reports of a floating island on the loch. The tourist trade gathered momentum in the later 18th century and flourished throughout the 19th under the stimulus of the writings of Sir Walter Scott. The loch remains one of Scotland's major tourist attractions, and an immensely popular area for day visitors from all over Central Scotland. The two main Visitor Centres are Lomond Shores at Balloch (open all year) and the National Park Gateway Centre at Balmaha (open Easter-October).

Balmaha–Rowardennan
(11.75 km; 7.25 miles)

THE line of the West Highland Way from Balmaha to the hotel at Rowardennan is never far from the shore of Loch Lomond, winding amiably up and down hill, into bays and round promontories, through open woodlands and dense conifer plantations. If for any reason you lose the route, it is only necessary to make your way back to the minor road that parallels the Way, and to follow it until you pick up the Way again. Great care should be exercised on the road, however; it is narrow and winding, with short steep hills and blind bends. In summer it becomes very busy and can be hazardous for pedestrians.

This section of the Way should not be hurried over, for its constantly changing scenery demands appreciation. The oakwoods are particularly rich in natural history interest, and there are many little gravel beaches and miniature headlands that offer ideal lunch spots or just an excuse for a rest on a sunny day.

It should be mentioned, in case you are tempted by a hot spell, that Loch Lomond has an ugly reputation as a trap for unwary bathers, and has claimed the lives of even strong and experienced swimmers. The shores are in places deceptively steep-shelving and the deeper waters are always chill, however invitingly warm the shallows may be. The loch is also liable to sudden sharp squalls of wind, perhaps caused by local funneling effects in the glens that run down to the loch. In 1829 one of these squalls struck a rowing boat in which the composer Felix Mendelssohn and a companion were crossing the loch, and came very close to upsetting it.

From Balmaha the Way sets off along the boardwalk between road and loch round the head of the bay. Where the road turns steeply uphill through the Pass of Balmaha, the Way carries on along the road to the old pier for a hundred metres or so before it, too, climbs steeply up to the right and back to the top of the hill, which goes by the curious name of Craigie Fort.

On the flat top you will again notice the rough Old Red Sandstone conglomerate that forms the ridge of Conic Hill and the line of islands from Inchcailloch to Inchmurrin. From this vantage point, formerly crowned by a cairn marking the official opening of the West Highland Way in 1980, you can gather a good impression of the character of the whole southern end of the loch. Above the wooded eastern shore Ben Lomond provides a challenging waymark.

Offshore lies a representative selection of the loch's islands: some large, some tiny, some almost flat, others rugged and high. Practically all of them were inhabited in the past, since they offered a refuge or a stronghold with a slightly higher degree of security in troubled times. Inchcailloch, the nearest — it looks only a stone's throw offshore — is typical in this respect. It is believed to have been the site of a nunnery in the early Christian era in Scotland. According to tradition, St Kentigerna, the mother of St Fillan who gave his name to Strath Fillan near Crianlarich, died on the island in 734AD. Later the church on lnchcailloch was the parish church of what is now Buchanan parish; in its graveyard are buried several members of the wild clans MacFarlane and MacGregor who controlled the lands around the upper part of Loch Lomond. The island was farmed until about 1770, when the Duke of Montrose ended the lease and allowed it to revert to woodland.

Because this southern part of the loch is so open and shallow, it has been known to freeze over in severe winters and on occasion the usual mailboat run to the islands has been performed on foot. In the 'Great Frost' of 1895 the ice cover was so thick and extensive that over 30,000 people came to walk, skate and curl on the loch. By contrast, it is unknown for the loch to freeze over north of Rowardennan.

From Craigie Fort, the Way heads briefly along the hilltop towards Conic Hill before dropping sharply down the further side of the hill through pleasant open oakwoods to the shore. It holds to the shore around Arrochymore Point to the car-park at Milarrochy. The exposures of rock at the edge of the loch are of considerable interest; contrary to expectations, beds of red sandstone outcrop here, north of the Highland Boundary Fault. These are the Upper Old Red Sandstones, laid down across the fault-line and later down-faulted, so that they have been preserved here while erosion has stripped them from the country south of the fault, where they stood higher. As the Way turns into Milarrochy Bay (car park and toilets) it crosses the northern limb of the Boundary Fault and passes into the major Highland formations, the Dalradian schists and grits.

At the back of the bay the West Highland Way takes to the road to avoid a private campsite on the shore. From Milarrochy Cottage it runs on the right-hand verge as far as the bridge on the Blair burn. Here it enters the Queen Elizabeth Forest Park, which stretches from Loch Lomond eastwards through the Trossachs and covers some 17,000 hectares (42,000 acres). The greater part of the oakwood on the land has been retained, and is now managed in consultation with Scottish Natural Heritage. The Way follows a pleasant path on the west side of the road, but screened from it by trees. It crosses the stream below Blair Cottage by its own little plank bridge, and goes up an open field to the edge of the plantations clothing Strathcashell Point. The path changes direction several times, but is always well marked. After 700 metres or so, the forest gives way to more open deciduous woodland. The route meanders gently downhill to rejoin the road opposite the Cashel Farm road-end. The 'Cashel' of these place names is a complex of grassed-over dykes and ditches near the Point, thought by archaeologists to be an Iron Age fortification.

Cashel Farm is now owned by the Royal Scottish Forestry Society. A major regeneration programme involving native trees is underway, and there are several good walks laid out.

The Way follows the road on the long straight past the campsite (with a useful shop) on the left, then clambers along a path on the verge and hillside as far as Anchorage Cottage. It is worth the effort to avoid the road, which is here squeezed between loch and hillside with little room for traffic and pedestrians. The slight extra elevation improves the view across the loch to the island of Inchlonaig and the woods and meadows of Luss on the opposite shore. Inchlonaig is notable for its yews, which tradition avers were planted on the instructions of Robert the Bruce to supply longbows for his archers, and for its fallow deer; the island was a private deer park of the Colquhouns of Luss from 1663.

At Anchorage Cottage the route takes the road again for a short distance to Sallochy, where it goes left towards the loch in fine open oakwoods. After a short stretch by the shore, it turns inland and climbs over a ridge to circumvent a steep rock rib that falls to the loch, barring passage by the shoreline. When the tree canopy is not too dense, this ridge gives an excellent view, with the abrupt narrowing of the loch at Ross Point standing in sharp contrast to the wide sweep of water and islands to the south. The route drops down to the north-west, returns to the shore, and continues along it for about 800 metres through splendid oakwoods to the car park by the bay.

The oakwoods that are Loch Lomond's crowning glory are no more than semi-natural. They are composed of both the standard British oaks, the sessile and the pedunculate, and many hybrids between them. This great hardwood resource was exploited in a remarkable range of ways from the 15th century on. At first, timber was cut for house-building and for the shipbuilding industry of Dumbarton. In the 17th century the oakwood provided the charcoal for ironsmelting in small local sites called 'bloomeries', until these were superseded in the later 18th century as iron production became concentrated in large-scale Lowland works using coal. Several bloomery sites have been identified up and down the loch's east shore by their characteristic mounds of purplish-black slag. You might come across a small site where bog ore was smelted almost anywhere below the tree line along the West Highland Way.

As the iron trade dwindled, the oak-bark industry which had complemented it came to the fore. The bark commanded a good price as a vital ingredient in the process of leather-tanning. Its production was based on a system of woodland management known as 'coppice-with-standards', in which the 'standard' tree was left to produce seed, while regenerating shoots were regularly thinned and the coppiced trees felled on a rotation of about 20 years. Thus in 1841 the Duke of Montrose ran a 25-year cycle on his 3000 acres of oakwood, cutting 120 acres each year. The bark was exported by water to Glasgow, Ireland and the West of England.

Beyond the car park the Way continues along the shore, passing between the Universities' Field Centre at Ross and its boat-house before striking steeply up into Ross Wood. Once on top of the hill, 73 metres (240 feet) above the loch, the route begins a long, gradual descent, giving occasional glimpses ahead of Ben Lomond rising broad-shouldered over its wooded lower slopes. After about 600 metres, the Way approaches the edge of open pasture land, but then goes leftwards through the woods again to the cottage and outbuildings by the burn, close to the bay below Coille Mhor. This is a peaceful, secluded spot.

If the water-level in the loch is low, the remains of a crannog may be visible not far offshore in the bay. There are several of these lake dwellings in Loch Lomond; they fulfilled the same defensive role as the islands did, but were man-made structures created by dumping boulders, brushwood and timber into the shallows by the edge of the loch to form a large platform on which huts to hold men and beasts could then be constructed. A causeway of timber or stone, just below water level and hence invisible to hostile visitors, was built to link the crannog to the shore. The best-preserved of the Loch Lomond crannogs is off Strathcashell Point; most of them now show only a few protruding boulders. It is thought that they were built in the Iron Age, but in some parts of Scotland they continued in use to the Middle Ages.

Beyond the stream the Way wanders along behind an alder swamp, crosses another burn, and climbs over a knoll in a deep, dark, hushed, needle-carpeted plantation of larch, from which it emerges abruptly at a little car

The loch shore near Rowardennan.

park above the inlet of Lochan Maoil Dhuinne. Beyond this inlet, the route returns to the lochshore in open oak wood which gradually thickens into a mixed plantation. The Way skirts most of this by working along above the rocky shoreline. After a few hundred metres, it turns inland and breaks out of the thicket on to the road just 300 metres south of the Rowardennan Hotel. You can find accommodation here, at the hotel and at the Youth Hostel some 750 metres (half a mile) further north, and transport: a passenger ferry runs to Inverbeg several times a day in summer, and there are also ferry links to Inversnaid, Luss and Balloch during the summer. There is no bus service back to Balmaha.

Rowardennan is also the starting-point of the path up Ben Lomond, one of Scotland's most-climbed and best-loved peaks, and since 1982 in the ownership of the National Trust for Scotland. The Ben is not only an important milepost on the West Highland Way, marking the first quarter of the route: it also has the distinction of being, at 974 metres (3195 feet), the most southerly of Scotland's Munros — the 284 mountains over 3000 feet (914 metres) listed originally by Sir Hugh Munro in 1891. By inference, therefore, it should be an exceptionally good viewpoint, and it is. In fair weather the ascent presents no difficulty, and can be thoroughly recommended as a fine half-day walk. This area is now known as the Ben Lomond Memorial Park (a park within a park), and is dedicated to the memory of those who fell in the two World Wars. There is a striking commemorative granite sculpture set on a small point which commands a superb view up the loch, just beyond the car park.

The facilities here include the car park, toilets and an interpretive display.

Ptarmigan and Ben Lomond from Rowardennan.

Looking across Loch Lomond

Rowardennan – Inverarnan

SUMMARY

Distance: 22.5km (14 miles). ~~24 k. ≃ 15.5~~

Height Range: 20-100m.

Terrain: By far the roughest section of the Way, particularly north of Inversnaid where the path makes a tortuous route along the side of Loch Lomond with many ups and downs. A full, hard day's walk but the scenery is superb.

Dogs are not allowed on the section from Pollochro to Beinglas Farm, even on a lead.

Opposite: Walking North from Rowardennan.

Rowardennan – Inversnaid

(11.75 km; 7.25 miles)

FROM Rowardennan to the head of Loch Lomond the West Highland Way holds to the eastern shore of the loch: sometimes close by the water's edge, sometimes well up the slopes. The first section, to the hotel and road-end at Inversnaid, is a traverse through woodland under the steep flanks of Ben Lomond. Between Ptarmigan Lodge and Rowchoish bothy there is a choice between a low-level route, picking its way through the lochshore oakwoods on a rough but scenic path, and a high-level route on the forest road, which gives easier and more straightforward walking. These optional routes rejoin about 500 metres beyond Rowchoish; thereafter an excellent path winds gradually down to the lochshore near Cailness and continues close above the loch by the wooded slopes of Craig Rostan to Inversnaid. In fine weather this is an idyllic walk through sun-dappled woods, with the loch glittering through the trees and a profusion of birdlife and bright, small flowers to add interest and colour.

A little way north of the Rowardennan Hotel, the public road ends at the large car park by the pier. There have long been proposals to push a road up the east shore of the loch at least as far as Inversnaid to complete a tourist circuit. This was strongly advocated by the minister of Buchanan parish in the New Statistical Account of Scotland in 1841, and proposed as relief work for the unemployed during the 1930s by Tom Johnston, later Secretary of State for Scotland. Happily, however, there is to date only the forest road to Rowchoish, and there seems little chance of that changing.

The Way follows the track up behind the car-park towards the Youth Hostel, but leaves it on the left and continues past the cabins at Ardess under the hill, which occupy the site of one of the larger bloomeries on the east shore of the loch. A kilometre or so further on, the road forks, the left-hand branch being the drive to Ptarmigan Lodge: the Way goes right on the forest road, which now begins its gradual climb to over 200 metres (650 feet), and passes the NTS ranger base.

Ptarmigan Lodge takes its name from the spur of Ben Lomond above, which had that name as long ago as Roy's Map of about 1750. The ptarmigan may still be seen occasionally on the slopes of Ben Lomond, though usually off the path to the summit where there is less disturbance. A cousin of the red grouse, it will often let you come close enough to admire its handsome mottled plumage, which in winter turns snowy-white, before gliding off a short distance.

Some 300 metres beyond the Ptarmigan Lodge junction, the Way itself divides. The low-level route descends by a flight of steps to the shore; the upper route continues on the Forestry Commission road, winding uphill through mixed plantations. The road provides easier and quicker walking, but it lacks much detailed interest and the outward views are generally very restricted, though it is worth looking back at intervals for the striking prospects down the loch.

The lochshore route, through woodland of oak and birch, is distinctly rough in places; the going may be steep above the loch, or scrambling by the water's edge among boulders and broken crags. However, there are no very fearsome obstacles to overcome, and there are many compensations by way of wildlife interest and human history. One of the bigger crags, about 2.5 km (1.5 miles) beyond Ptarmigan Lodge, goes by the name of Rob Roy's Prison; here, it is said, he kept hostages and kidnap victims in a natural rock cell close above the loch. As with Rob Roy's Cave, north of Inversnaid, there must be some doubt as to whether Rob Roy ever used his 'prison', but this is certainly the beginning of his country; the lands of Craig Rostan from about here to the head of the loch were his property. Indeed at the beginning of the 18th century, Rob Roy and his MacGregor kinsmen held most of the territory from Loch Lomond east to Strathyre, and from Aberfoyle north to Glen Dochart.

The history of the Clan Gregor in general, and of Rob Roy in particular, has been so much romanticised and coloured by Sir Walter Scott and other writers that it is often difficult to distinguish fact from fiction. As far as it is known, the real history of the MacGregors is dramatic enough. In the 13th century they occupied the lands of Glen Strae and Glen Orchy at the head of Loch

Awe, but fell foul of the expansionist strategy of the Campbells, who were able to use legal means to dispossess the MacGregors and drive them eastwards. The clan's subsequent history is one of occupying disputed lands, oppressed by powerful neighbours, and surviving by their wits, force of arms, and a good deal of cattle-thieving over the Highland line, later formalised, as already mentioned, into an efficient system of blackmail.

The MacGregors seem to have had an unhappy knack of backing the wrong side in a conflict, or attacking the wrong neighbours, a talent exploited by their enemies. At the beginning of the reign of Mary, Queen of Scots they took part in an abortive rebellion, and 'letters of fire and sword' were issued against the clan. In 1603 they massacred the Colquhouns in the Battle of Glen Fruin on the west side of Loch Lomond, and these letters were renewed and the name of MacGregor proscribed, the use of the surname being forbidden on pain of death.

This history explains much of the character and life-style of Rob Roy. The by-name Roy, from the Gaelic *ruadh*, he owed to his red hair. He was born in 1671 into one of the cadet families of the MacGregor chiefs, and by the time he was 30 he had shown his mettle by leading raids into the Lowlands, including the notorious Her'ship of Kippen, in which he carried off large numbers of cattle. He had married Mary, daughter of Gregor of Comer, under the north-eastern flanks of Ben Lomond; he had gained by gift or purchase the lands of Inversnaid and Craig Rostan; and he was established as a large-scale cattle dealer and drover. Shortly thereafter he became tutor to his 13-year-old nephew, the seventh Chief of the Glen Gyle MacGregors, and was thus effectively acting head of the clan.

The more lawless part of Rob Roy's career began in 1711, when his droving business crashed after his head drover absconded with all the cash for the spring purchase of cattle; two of his chief debtors fled at the same time. The Duke of Montrose, Rob Roy's main creditor and for long an ally and confederate, had him first bankrupted and then outlawed; his house at Craig Rostan was burnt and his wife and family evicted. Rob Roy took to the hills,

Opposite: In the Loch Lomond Oakwoods.

and began a long campaign of reiving against Montrose. In 1716 he captured his factor on his rounds and carried him off — some say to the Prison. Unfortunately the Duke was reluctant to ransom his servant, and he was eventually released, minus the rents he had collected.

In his later years Rob Roy seems to have led a more settled life, and died in his bed at Inverlochlarig near Balquhidder in 1734. Two of his sons carried forward his less reputable activities till 1750, when they overstepped the mark by abducting a supposedly rich widow from Balfron and forcibly marrying her to one of their own number, Robin Oig. The authorities were no longer prepared to tolerate such excesses, and more importantly, were in a position to suppress them. The brothers were pursued and broken, and the hanging of Robin Oig in 1754 marked the effective end of the MacGregors' wild career.

From the vicinity of the Prison northwards, there are superb views west through the Arrochar-Tarbet gap to the hills above Loch Long. The spectacular *piece de resistance* in these views is the Cobbler, otherwise known as Ben Arthur; its craggy triple peaks make it a favourite haunt of Glasgow climbers. The pass between Loch Long and Loch Lomond, probably cut during the last Ice Age by a branch of the Loch Lomond glacier, is only a little over 30 metres (100 feet) above sea level, and may have been used in centuries past as a regular portage for small boats. The Gaelic name Tarbet implies a 'boatdrag', but by association it has come to be applied to any isthmus. This was certainly the route taken by Viking raiders in 1263, when forces under King Haakon were massed in the Clyde to assert Viking authority over western Scotland and the Hebrides. Haakon was eventually thwarted at the Battle of Largs, but not before a raiding squadron of perhaps 40 longships had been dragged over from Loch Long to Loch Lomond, where they wrought havoc along the Lennox shore and on the islands, pillaging and burning.

Beyond the Prison, the lower route continues along the loch to where a spur track descends to the shore from the forest road above. The path then leads uphill through conifers by a miniature glen to Rowchoish. The bothy, off the path on the left a little beyond the crest, is almost invisible among the trees until you are within a few metres of it. It was restored to provide a basic shelter by the Forestry Commission and the Scottish Rights of Way Society as a memorial to William Ferris, a dynamic out-door enthusiast from Glasgow. From the 1920s to his death in 1963, Willie Ferris was enormously active in outdoor organisations. Among much else he was a founder of the Rucksack Club from which the SYHA evolved; he founded the Scottish Ramblers Federation; and he was a director and chairman of the Rights of Way Society. As he was a great devotee of Loch Lomond, the bothy is a particularly apt memorial for him.

The remains of stone walls around the bothy are mute testimony to depopulation. There were nine families at Rowchoish in 1759, and at least three more settlements between here and Inversnaid, on a stretch of the shore where there is now only one cottage.

In good weather Rowchoish is an ideal place for rest and reflection. The view across the loch to the 'Arrochar Alps' is inspiring; the view north up the loch is inviting and stimulating. There is a glimpse of Inversnaid on the wooded east shore, and a distant prospect of the next mountain milepost, Beinn Dubhchraig, which appears as a flattened pyramid beyond the head of the loch. Since Beinn Dubhchraig and its neighbours, Beinn Oss and Beinn Lui, stand near the mid-point of the West Highland Way, and are high enough to be seen from a considerable distance, they are a particularly useful gauge of progress.

From Rowchoish the low-level route climbs gently through damp woodlands to rejoin the upper route on the forest road, only to have the road dwindle away after a few hundred metres. It gives way to a delightful little path that winds through pleasant woods of birch, oak and pine for a while before descending to the northern boundary of the Forest Park, close by the lochshore at the Cailness Burn. On the other side of the burn, under the hill, the trim farm cottage of Cailness commands a royal vista over open pastures to the loch and the mountains of the opposite shore. The Cailness Burn has something of a turbulent recent history, with footbridges having been washed away twice: first in 1975 and again in 1985.

The 1975 flood is commemorated by a cairn erected by members of staff from Cardonald College, Glasgow, whose colleague Bill Lobban lost his life trying to save one of a party of students involved in a field exercise. The accident happened on 23 November 1975, when the group were crossing the burn and a member of the party slipped. Bill managed to save the student but in doing so was swept into the loch.

The West Highland Way carries on along the lochshore as a well-marked trail. Generally it gives pleasant, easy walking though it runs under and among broken crags of contorted mica-schists. This wooded stretch of lochside is very popular with birdwatchers. The high density and variety of birdlife in the oak and birch woods will be obvious even to the uninitiated. A few of the birds are conspicuous by their size and bright colouring, like the jay and the green woodpecker, both of which are here close to the northern limit of their breeding range. Some announce themselves by their call, like the cuckoo, or like the great spotted woodpecker, by its drumming on trees. Many, however, are small and rather shy, such as the tiny treecreeper, which may be seen scurrying furtively up the trunks of oaks, picking at insects in the bark. It is worth sitting quietly for five or ten minutes simply to see what will appear.

The path arrives almost unexpectedly at Inversnaid, crossing the Snaid Burn just above its celebrated waterfall and descending sharply to the car-park, pier and large Victorian hotel. The summer bustle of Inversnaid comes as a curious intermission in the Way's progress up the wild east shore of Loch Lomond. It occurs as a result of the presence here of the one low break in the hills of the east shore: the road from Aberfoyle comes through a pass at only 150 metres (500 feet) by Loch Arklet. Geologists have suggested that this remarkable break is a remnant of the pre-glacial drainage patterns, when a river rising in the Arrochar hills flowed east across the present line of Loch Lomond, eventually to join the Forth. As evidence for their theory they point out the close alignment of the Inveruglas Water with the Arklet valley, and the 'hanging valley' character of the Snaid burn, with its steep-sided glen and waterfalls, suggesting that its direction of flow may have been reversed as a result of glacial erosion.

It was to cover this low pass, and thus to keep in check the activities of the MacGregors, that the Garrison of Inversnaid was built in 1718-19. The MacGregors did not take kindly to this intrusion on their lands, as they saw it. One night in August 1718 they kidnapped eight masons and quarriers from the site of the barracks and carried them off to the Lowlands before releasing them. Nevertheless the work reached completion in the following year, and the barracks were actively garrisoned until they were seized by the MacGregors during the 1745 Rising. General Wolfe of Quebec fame is said to have served here as a young officer. The site of the barracks, and a few remains, can be seen a kilometre or so up the road towards Loch Arklet, though most of the stonework is incorporated into the buildings of Garrison Farm.

A post-bus service connects Inversnaid to Aberfoyle, but for most destinations it is easier and quicker to take the ferry over to Inveruglas and the west shore road, or in summer the ferry to Rowardennan, Luss or Balloch.

Because of its salient position, particularly for the 19th-century tourist traffic through Loch Lomond and the Trossachs, Inversnaid has if anything a slightly over-worked reputation as a beauty spot, and a plethora of literary associations. The Wordsworths and Coleridge came here more than once in the course of their adventurous Highland tour of 1803; at the Inversnaid ferry-house they encountered the 'sweet Highland girl' lauded in one of Wordsworth's less successful poems.

Nearly 80 years later the Jesuit poet Gerard Manley Hopkins, with a sensitive vision sharpened, perhaps, by his missionary work in a squalid area of Glasgow, caught the spirit of the Inversnaid burn and wove it into a plea on behalf of wild nature:

'This darksome burn, horseback brown,
His rollrock highroad roaring down,
In coop and in comb the fleece of his foam
Flutes and low to the lake falls home…

…What would the world be, once bereft
Of wet and of wildness? Let them be left,
O let them be left, wildness and wet;
Long live the weeds and the wilderness yet.'

Inversnaid – Inverarnan

(10.5 km; 6.5 miles)

THE section of the Way from Inversnaid to the foot of Glen Falloch is undoubtedly the roughest part of the whole route, but it is also one of the finest. The east shore of Loch Lomond falls in a steep, broken, thickly wooded slope to the loch, which here lies deep and narrow where the glaciers have gouged out the valley bottom to over 150 metres below sea level. From Rob Roy's Cave north for about 3 km (2 miles) much of the Way crosses wooded slopes close above the water's edge, with a good deal of strenuous up-and-down work: you should allow plenty of time for this stretch. A great deal of improvement work has been carried out, difficult sections have been smoothed over, and the path is now much easier than it once was, but one or two places still call for care, particularly with a pack on or in wet weather. Good boots are essential for this section. The difficulties, such as they are, end where the Way leaves the lochshore about a kilometre south of Doune.

It is quite straightforward to avoid this section if you are deterred by the prospect: simply take the ferry over from Inversnaid to Inveruglas, and walk or catch the bus northwards on the west shore road to rejoin the Way at Beinglas Farm beyond the head of the loch.

However, the glorious roughness of the lochshore and the wildness of the woodland along the Way should not readily be missed. Because this area is so rugged it is relatively little visited and has a particularly rich flora and fauna. There are wild goats hereabouts, as further south by Ben Lomond, and even if you do not see them you may catch a whiff of their distinct musty odour. There is a special piquancy in the isolation of this part of the Way, sharpened by the hum of traffic on the A82 on the other side of the loch — at some points only a few hundred metres away, but in another world of human activity.

The footpath north from Inversnaid (now part of an RSPB reserve) is well-worn and popular as far as Rob Roy's Cave, and along the way you can enjoy superb tree-framed views across the loch to the Arrochar hills and the

Opposite: Mountain and loch combine in scenic grandeur.

wooded slopes behind Inveruglas. Nathaniel Hawthorne, the American author, came here in 1857 and was firmly of the opinion that 'this particular stretch of Loch Lomond, in front of Inversnaid, is the most beautiful lake and mountain view that I have ever seen'.

The scene has been changed somewhat since Hawthorne's visit by the creation of the Loch Sloy hydro-electric scheme, which has largest generating capacity of all Scotland's conventional hydro schemes. The head of water is 274 metres (900 feet) and the catchment area, originally very small, was substantially enlarged by tunneling and diversion works. Being so near the west coast, it is a good catchment for rainfall. Way-walkers might prefer not to know that Loch Sloy holds the Scottish record for maximum rainfall in 24 hours - 238.4 mm (9.39 inches) on 17 January 1974. The dam itself is hidden behind Ben Vorlich, but the downfall pipes running down to the power station at Inveruglas are conspicuous on the hill-front.

'Loch Sloy' was the watchword and battle-cry of the Clan MacFarlane who occupied the west shore of the loch north of Tarbet, and who had a castle on the small wooded island in Inveruglas bay. Like their MacGregor neighbours, the MacFarlanes had a bad reputation as raiders and cattle thieves.

It is about a kilometre north from Inversnaid to Rob Roy's Cave. It is not a cave at all in the strict sense, being just a deep crevice in the mass of enormous fallen blocks under Sroin Uaidh. You may have some difficulty in finding it, as there are quite a few crannies and corners in the chaos of rock, and you should take care of your footing, particularly in wet conditions, when mica-schist can become as slippy as ice. Once you find the right crevice there is no mistaking it, as a well-meaning enthusiast has daubed 'CAVE' in large white letters over the right-hand wall.

Given Rob Roy's association with this area, and the fact that his house was burnt by his enemies on more than one occasion, it is quite possible that he may have used the cave for shelter. In earlier days, however, it was known as King Robert's Cave, in the belief that Bruce had used it in 1306 while a fugitive after his successive defeats at Methven and Dalrigh. There must, however, be a suspicion that both associations flow from the same deep romantic springs that have cluttered the Western Highlands with a surfeit of nooks called 'Bonnie Prince Charlie's Cave'.

The whole of the Loch Lomond area acquired an exalted romantic stature from the novels and poetry of Sir Walter Scott. His impact is epitomised in Dorothy Wordsworth's two visits to the cave: in 1803 she came alone but for her brother and Coleridge; in 1822, four years after the publication of Scott's *Rob Roy*, she was accompanied by a large party from the loch steamer. A piper, a token Ancient Highlander, and boys selling bags of nuts were in attendance. Her fellow-tourists rushed to enter the cave, emerging to declare 'Well! there is nothing

The Way rises high above the loch.

to be seen; but it is worth while, if only to say that one has been there!'

Beyond Rob Roy's Cave the sense of wildness quickly closes around the Way again. The path clambers up and down from the lochshore gravel to boggy flats, through high bracken and oakwood, under crags and fallen trees. This country is not much visited and little grazed by animals. It displays a fascinating range of woodland and bog flowers, and a wide variety of woodland birds. As counter to the foreground detail there are occasional views over the loch to the steep, bluff slopes of Ben Vorlich, shaggy with birchwood, and glimpses ahead to the next two mountain mileposts, Beinn Oss and Beinn Dubhchraig, gradually drawing nearer over the head of the loch on its western side.

As elsewhere in Scotland, the wilderness quality of this area is more apparent than real. Under Creag an Fhithich you will find the remains of the croft of Pollochro, now marked by three great sycamores and a rickle of stones on a boggy flat, but listed as an inhabited house in the 17th century and occupied within the century past.

As you approach the Allt Rostan, the little, densely-wooded island called 'Island I Vow' will catch your attention. The curious name is a hopeless corruption of a Gaelic name — an old anglicisation was 'Ylenow'. There is a ruin on the island, thought variously to have been a nunnery, a castle of the MacFarlanes, and a private house. Such is the history of Loch Lomond that it may well have been all these at different times.

A short distance beyond the Allt Rostan the Way crosses a precipitous waterfall slab by a bridge perched virtually above the waters of the loch; the ascent and descent either side of the bridge are steep, and require a little care. A few hundred metres more of walking on the wooded slope, and the Way emerges on to the open gravel shore by the bay south of Doune — a pleasant and sunny spot for lunch or a break. The going from here on is perfectly straightforward. The Way crosses the little stream that enters the bay and strikes uphill and slightly leftwards to keep to open ground over the hill to Doune. The network of dykes and the larch plantation on the hilltop convey a pleasant sense of domesticity contrasting with the rough country that the Way has come through. Doune Farm, long derelict, has now been restored, while the outbuilding 40 metres east of the house has been reconstructed by the Mountain Bothies Association as a bothy for Way walkers and other outdoor folk — a welcome haven in a superb situation, looking north to the head of the loch.

The Way returns to the lochshore briefly as it continues towards Ardleish, but the slopes are gentle and the walking easy. Below Ardleish a signal hoist offers the opportunity to summon and hire a ferry-boat from Ardlui for any walkers who feel their efforts on the Way have earned them a short trip to the facilities available across the loch. The Way continues uphill, passing above Ardleish farm; it crosses the burn and follows an old pathway on the west side of the little gorge above, to the marshy col at its head, where it crosses to pass the eastern shore of the reedy Dubh Lochan.

The crest of the col is a superlative viewpoint, and effectively marks the end of the Loch Lomond section of the West Highland Way. Behind, the loch twists southwards between wooded promontories, with Ben Lomond a sharp cone peering over the craggy ridge of Craig Rostan. To the north the trinity of milepost mountains is completed as Beinn Lui appears to join Beinn Oss and Beinn Dubhchraig: all three now look comparatively close, soaring over the moors above Glen Falloch. Beyond the secret little valley of the Dubh Lochan, the path holds its height for a few hundred metres on a grassy shelf dotted with the broken walls of a ruined clachan, before running downhill to the foot of Glen Falloch. The glen in its lower part is a deep-cut, flat-floored glacial trench; its tributary valleys are good examples of 'hanging valleys', and after rain the waterfalls on the western flank are a fine spectacle.

The path descends gently, winding through woods, to emerge on the flats a short distance south of the Ben Glas Burn. A curious feature that you may notice as you descend is the Inverarnan canal, a short channel dug about 1850 to allow pleasure craft on Loch Lomond to bring their passengers right up to the Inverarnan hotel. Overhead, the transmission lines carrying power to and from the big pumped-storage hydro scheme of Cruachan, near Loch Awe, swoop across the valley.

This section ends at the bridge on the Ben Glas Burn, by the substantial ruin of the old Beinglas farm. Above the bridge the burn plunges nearly 300 metres in a kilometre over a series of fine falls which can be awesome in wet weather. Unfortunately the best of the falls cannot be seen from the Way, as it is too close under the hill; to appreciate their full height you must follow the short access branch of the Way leading round by the burn to the bridge over the Falloch, and so to the A82 main road. Beinglas Farm has the second pair of wooden wigwams, each sleeping four people, and also two 'shielings', an alternative design.

Four hundred metres down the road stands the hotel at Inverarnan, an ancient cattle-drovers' inn on the route from Argyll and the West round the head of Loch Lomond to the Lowland markets at Crieff or Falkirk. The cattle were driven over the hills from Glen Fyne - you will see the 'lairig' names signifying a pass on the map - and then up the Ben Glas Burn into the Balquhidder or Glen Gyle valleys. In the 19th century, like many of its counterparts, the inn became a tourist hotel and the canal link with Loch Lomond was made. Nathaniel Hawthorne, whose favourable impressions of Inversnaid were mentioned earlier, also came to Inveraman in 1857, and encountered the kind of weather that is all too common in the Highlands:

> 'these clouds came down and enveloped us in a drizzle, or rather a shower, of such minute drops that they had not weight enough to fall. This, I suppose, was a genuine Scotch mist; and as such it is well enough to have experienced it, though I would willingly never see it again'.

From the 1880s the Inverarnan Hotel became a well-known centre for climbers, and its hospitality was almost legendary. During the 1930s it was a favourite base of the Glasgow section of the Junior Mountaineering Club of Scotland. The author and mountaineer W. H. Murray tells a tale of how he and two companions, having abandoned a January trip to Glen Coe in appalling weather, made a nefarious entry to the hotel in the small hours of the morning by forcing a window. They found a bed big enough for three - 'the bridal suite, no doubt' - and slept undisturbed till noon. He does not relate what the proprietors said when they heard of the exploits of these midwinter 'honeymooners'.

There is a restaurant, the Stagger Inn, opposite the hotel. Three kilometres (1.9 miles) further south on the A82 road (but also accessible by ferry from Ardleish, as mentioned above) Ardlui offers a hotel, campsite, and shop, as well as railway and bus services both northwards and southwards. Ben Vorlich is a straightforward climb from near the hotel, and gives an excellent retrospective view of this section of the West Highland Way.

In Glen Falloch.

Inverarnan – Crianlarich

SUMMARY

Distance: 10.5km (6.5 miles).

Height Range: 40-200m.

Terrain: A short, pleasant section through Glen Falloch on good paths. The Way bypasses Crianlarich to the west but a spur path leads into the village, the halfway point on the route.

Dogs are not allowed in this section, even on a lead.

Breadalbane

FROM the head of Loch Lomond the West Highland Way continues northwards by Glen Falloch, Strath Fillan and upper Glen Orchy to the southern edge of Rannoch Moor. Between these valleys, the Way crosses and re-crosses the main east-west watershed of the Highlands. It is therefore appropriate to call this chapter Breadalbane, for this title, another historic division of Scotland, is generally taken to be a compound of *braghad*, the Gaelic for an 'upper part', or the higher part of a slope, and Alban, the ancient name for Scotland, and hence means the upland of Scotland.

Strictly speaking, the name Breadalbane should be applied to the country in and around the valleys of the three great parallel tributaries of the Tay: Glen Lyon, Glen Lochay and Glen Dochart. But for the purpose of this guide, it is not unreasonable to extend the boundaries of the province, for Glen Orchy and Glen Falloch both had vital links with the Earldom of Breadalbane, a powerful force in Scotland's history. Indeed, the family line of the Earls first sprang from the Campbells of Glenorchy, who gradually, by fair means and foul, extended their lands and power at the expense of neighbouring clans like the MacGregors till they achieved the Earldom in 1677. The first Earl was particularly notorious for his devious self-seeking, and was implicated in the Massacre of Glen Coe. One of his contemporaries described him as being 'cunning as a fox, wise as a serpent, but as slippery as an eel'.

As part of their 'empire building', the Campbells bought the estate of Glenfalloch in 1599. A cadet branch of the family held the land and style of Glenfalloch till 1867, when on the demise of the senior lines of succession, William Campbell of Glenfalloch became sixth Earl of Breadalbane. Under his son, the third Marquis, the Breadalbane estates reached their greatest extent, stretching in a great belt from Aberfeldy to the west coast islands of Luing and Seil and totalling over 160,000 hectares (400,000 acres). In his comprehensive study *In Famed Breadalbane* the Rev. William Gillies quotes a pithy verse about these vast landholdings:

From Kenmore
To Ben Mohr
The land is a' the Markiss's;
The mossy howes, The heathery knowes, An' ilka
  bonnie park is his.
The bearded goats,
The toozie stots,
An' a' the braxy carcasses;
Ilk crofter's rent, ilk tinker's tent, An' ilka collie's
  bark is his.
The muircock's craw,
The piper's blaw,
The gillie's hard day's wark is his;
From Kenmore To Ben Mohr, the Warld is a' the
  Markiss's!

After the death of the Marquis in 1922, however, death duties caused the dismemberment of these great estates: Glen Falloch and Glen Orchy have passed into other hands.

Much of Breadalbane is deer and sheep country, with cattle-rearing on the valley floors, but in recent years there has been considerable afforestation, largely by the Forestry Commission. The natural history of the country evolves with the woodland; as the ground is ploughed and planted, the birds of grassland and heather moor, the lark and the pipit, the curlew, plover, and grouse, give way to willow-warblers, finches and tits. Fencing to exclude sheep and deer allows grass to grow more thickly, encouraging mice and voles, which in turn enlarges the scope for predators on the ground, like stoats and weasels, and in the air, like kestrels and short-eared owls.

In woodland or moorland the great scavenger is the 'hoodie', or hooded crow, readily identified by its grey back and underparts and its generally villainous demeanour; its breeding range extends as far south as the Highland edge, but it interbreeds with the common, carrion crow a good deal. Buzzards are not uncommon, and may be mistaken for the golden eagle until a genuine eagle appears, when the difference in size, shape, and flight becomes evident; but the chances of seeing eagles are not as good here as further north along the West Highland Way.

Overleaf: Wigwam shelter at Beinglas Farm.

Inverarnan – Crianlarich
(10.5 km; 6.5 miles)

FROM the head of Loch Lomond the Way runs up Glen Falloch and over a low pass to Crianlarich in Strath Fillan. The River Falloch is the dominant element throughout; from Beinglas Farm (where there is a campsite with small shop, and the wooden wigwam shelters) the route follows the east side of the river for nearly 4.75 km to Derrydaroch, crosses it, and holds to its west bank for another kilometre before climbing to join the old military road above the A82 trunk road. The old road takes the Way on to Crianlarich and gives wide views of the open upper glen and the mountains among which the Falloch has its sources.

To join the West Highland Way from the Inverarnan Hotel, go north up the A82 road for a few hundred metres, cross the Falloch by the bridge over to Beinglas, and turn sharp right to follow the bank of the river and the Ben Glas Burn to the footbridge. From this bridge the Way goes along behind Beinglas Farm, following a farm track northwards. Almost from the outset there is a sense of enclosure in the valley bottom, with restricted views that are characteristic of the lower part of Glen Falloch. A little over a kilometre from the farm the mood changes. The glen now runs up towards the north-east, with open moorland flanks. The river surges in wide, low falls over a rocky bar; the Way starts its steady ascent out of the Loch Lomond basin.

From here on till the Way leaves it, the Falloch is a long and splendid succession of gorges, rocky rapids, short cascades, cauldrons and wide dark pools, with short stretches of smooth water between. In wet weather it can be an awesome sight, but beware of venturing too close on the slippery schists of the banks. Geologists suggest that this spectacular course is a product of the complex history of drainage diversion in the Loch Lomond basin during and after the Pleistocene Ice Age. According to one theory, the Falloch and all its tributaries north from the Ardlui area previously drained north-eastwards to join the River Fillan, and thence the Tay, in the vicinity of present-day Crianlarich. Even after thousands of years, it seems that the river is still adjusting its course to a new line of flow.

On its progress up the Falloch the Way constantly moves from birch, alder and oak woodland to open pasture, and back again. Among the trees the going can be fairly rough, giving a sense of wildness entirely at variance with the occasional glimpses of traffic on the road or railway only a short distance away across the river.

There was an odd little skirmish in Glen Falloch in November 1845. At that time, during the height of the great railway mania that swept Britain, several proposals were mooted for routes through this area. The Duke of Montrose, a director of the proposed Caledonian Northern Direct line, sent a survey party into Glen Falloch, the property of the Marquis of Breadalbane, himself a director of the rival Scottish Grand Junction. When news of the trespass reached Breadalbane country, a body of men, mostly miners from the lead mines at Tyndrum, came down the glen, overwhelmed the CND party, and threw them and their theodolite into the ditch. In the event, their efforts proved superfluous, as the mania burned itself out shortly afterwards; it was another 45 years before the West Highland line was built through the glen.

On the open stretches, particularly opposite the Fionn Ghleann, you may catch a glimpse of one or all of the three big milepost Munros to the northwest: Beinn Dubhchraig, Beinn Oss and Beinn Lui. These give a fine long hill-walk, but are better taken from the Strath Fillan side. From the same area you should look for the great boulder called Clach-na-Briton, 'the stone of the Britons', on the slope of Cruachan Cruinn above the glen. This huge rock is supposed to have marked the boundary between the territories of the Britons, the Scots and the Picts during the Dark Ages.

The path continues to Derrydaroch. The name means 'the oak grove', and there are some oaks by the river, though pines are increasingly the dominant tree in the upper parts of the glen. These pines, scattered along the lower slopes of the valley sides, are a remnant of the old Wood of Caledon, the great pine forest that clothed the central part of the Highlands in the post-glacial period. Burning, grazing and felling for timber, perhaps in conjunction with climatic changes inhibiting natural regeneration, have gradually reduced the forest to the present widely dispersed fragments. Two larger remnant woods can be seen near the West Highland Way a little further north. These pine woods were the original habitat of the native red squirrel; you are more likely to see it here than on Loch Lomondside, where the introduced grey squirrel has effectively taken over the deciduous woods. This section of woodland is now fenced off and under active management to encourage regeneration.

The Way crosses the Falloch at the Derrydaroch bridge and turns sharp right over a birchwood knoll to return to the riverside. About a kilometre north from the bridge, the route climbs from the river to pass under the railway by a low-roofed cattle creep — an awkward passage if you are carrying a big pack. It passes under the A82 road by a tunnel, a short distance north of Carmyle Cottage, and strikes directly uphill for about 100 metres to join the old military road running under the electricity transmission line. The old road, an obvious grassy pathway, continues northwards along the hillside, and leads the Way the rest of the distance to Crianlarich.

The system of military roads in Highland Scotland was created largely in response to the Jacobite risings of 1715 and 1745. In the first great burst of activity, about 400 km were built under the command of Major General George Wade, who first identified the need for improved communications to pacify the area in his report on the state of the Highlands in 1724. During the ten years after 1725 Wade's main efforts were concentrated in the Central Highlands and Great Glen, linking the major Hanoverian forts and barracks in those areas.

It was left to Wade's successor as 'roadman', Major William Caulfeild, to fill out the skeleton of the road network. Between 1746 and 1767 Caulfeild directed the construction of over 1300 km of roads in Scotland, including all the sections now used by the West Highland Way, although a good part of his work was outwith the Highlands, in the North-East and Galloway. Despite this, Wade tends to get the credit for all the roads; as the well-known couplet has it:

> 'If you had seen these roads before they were made,
> You would hold up your hands and bless General
>   Wade.'

The roads were military not only in purpose but also in construction; they were built largely by troops, who earned double pay for the work, with a few civilian masons to help with the bridgeworks. The techniques employed were basic: a road-bed was cut by excavation on flat ground or by benching on slopes; the spoil was heaped into banks on either side, and the paving was built up in layers of gravel, the material getting smaller in successive layers. Cross-drains were usually open and stone-lined; culverts were a later sophistication. All the materials used were local, causing the civilian population to complain that the roads tended to run between ready sources of gravel, rather than following the route most convenient to peaceful travellers.

The old road gives wide views over upper Glen Falloch to the Crianlarich hills. The south-western peaks are characterised by long spurs radiating from craggy, knobbly tops; but a little further north along the Way, Ben More begins to appear as a massive, steep pyramid beyond the ridges of Cruach Ardrain. At 1174 metres the 'big ben' is the 15th highest mountain in Britain, and since its northern slope surges in one great sweep to the summit from the floor of Glen Dochart at about 170 metres, it shows its height to full advantage. In good conditions the view from the cairn is magnificent, and takes in much of the Central Highlands.

The Way continues above Keilator Farm, following the upper side of the dyke that encloses the improved ground. As a settlement Keilator pre-dates the military road; in a 17th century manuscript the name is listed as 'Chuletyr', suggesting that it may mean 'the nook on the slope'. Beyond the house and farm buildings, dyke and Way together run into the head of a little glen and follow it upwards. This deep-cut miniature valley is probably a former glacial melt-water channel by which dammed-up water escaped from Strath Fillan into Glen Falloch, perhaps at a period when the lower col a little to the east, now occupied by the main road and railway, was choked by ice. It goes by the name of Bogle Glen, a bogle being a Scots ghost, ghoul or goblin, but tradition is silent on the origin of the name.

At the narrow head of the glen the Way passes from the Loch Lomond drainage system into that of the Tay, from

the Atlantic side of Scotland to the North Sea side. This notable watershed is marked by a deer-fence and a gate protecting the Forestry Commission plantation to the north. Beyond the forest fence the route divides: the Way proper slants uphill, leftwards to a knoll above a little crag, well worth visiting for its wide view up and down Strath Fillan with the fine company of mountains that stand over it. Many walkers will, however, want to follow the spur path to Crianlarich to find accommodation, refreshments, supplies or transport. A choice lies between continuing on the old military road down to the A82, 700 metres west of the village, or following the pathway down towards the road just north of the station and youth hostel.

Crianlarich has the particular interest for Way-walkers of being roughly at the halfway point on the West Highland Way. The origin of its name is open to dispute though *craobh an lairig* - the tree by the pass - seems plausible. The historic origins of the settlement are uncertain too, since although Crianlarich now stands at the junction of both road and railway, it is already clear that the junction of the military road was some distance away; the site is a restricted one, between the morainic deposits on the pass and the ill-drained floodplain of Strath Fillan. In any event, Crianlarich owes much of its present character to its railway links and the subsequent tourist trade.

In common with Tyndrum, a few kilometres further up the valley, it long had the distinction of possessing two railway stations - the Lower station, on the Callander and Oban line, which ran along the south side of Glen Dochart and Strath Fillan, and which opened in 1873; and the Upper, on the West Highland line, which comes up Glen Falloch to cross Strath Fillan to its northern flank, opened in 1897. The two lines were controlled by the Caledonian and North British companies respectively, and as these were bitter rivals there was a minimum of co-operation between them. A linking spur (which crosses the road at the west end of the village) was built in 1897, but it was not used at all for several years, and never used to connect trains until after railway nationalisation. The Lower

Opposite: The River Cononish.

station was closed in 1965 when the Callander and Oban line was blocked by a landslide in Glen Ogle, to the east.

Crianlarich is still a centre of communications, with rail and bus services to Glasgow, Oban and Fort William as well as a post-bus service eastwards to Killin, Callander and Stirling. The village is equipped with shops, tearooms, post office and police station with a mountain rescue post. Accommodation includes a hotel, a youth hostel, and bed and breakfast in scattered houses westwards along the A82, but is should be borne in mind that it is a popular touring centre during the summer. Several establishments, including the hotel, tend to cater for the touring trade in preference to walkers - keep an eye out for the Walkers Welcome symbol if in doubt.

Because of its accessibility and the big hills around it, Crianlarich has long been a Mecca for hill walkers. Many Scottish mountaineers who learned their hillcraft in this area hold its highly individual Munros in great affection. Anyone with time in hand can profitably spend two or three days here, since a dozen or more fine hills can be reached from Crianlarich in a summer day's walking. There is a good deal of broken crag on these hills, and they demand respect and route-finding skills, particularly in misty and wet conditions, but still more so in winter or spring when rocks may be ice-glazed and snow-slopes hard-frozen. The shoulder of Ben More facing Crianlarich and the steep north-eastern aspect of Cruach Ardrain are notoriously dangerous in winter. In those conditions ice-axe and crampons, and skill in their use, are vital: and this is true of most of the bigger hills from here on northwards.

Approaching Tyndrum.

Crianlarich – Bridge of Orchy

SUMMARY

Distance: 21.5km (13 miles).

Height Range: 120-300m.

Terrain: Good paths and tracks with some moderate ascent and descent, but nothing unduly difficult and nowhere far from services. A straightforward day of glen and low pass walking amid outstanding mountain scenery.

Dogs are not allowed on the section through Kirkton Farm.

Crianlarich — Tyndrum
(10.5 km; 6.5 miles)

IN its progress up Strath Fillan the West Highland Way takes a pleasantly serendipitous course, first in the forest plantations on the southern slopes of the valley, then across the river and over farmland on its north side, and latterly by open moorland to Tyndrum. The strath has a particular charm in running among high mountains and moors, but retaining much of the atmosphere of a lowland valley.

From Crianlarich the best way back onto the route is to retrace your steps on one of the spur routes. For guidance there is a waymarker and sign in the small car park across the road from the station. The Forestry Commission ploughing and planting in this area took place about the same time as the creation and marking of the Way, so that the opportunity was taken to integrate the route into the planting programme. A wide variety of species was planted, and breaks left at strategic points to provide maximum interest and amenity for walkers.

From the rocky knoll above the old military road the Way trends north-northwest, climbing gradually and commanding fine views back over Crianlarich to Ben More and Stob Binnein, and across the valley to Ben Challum on its north side. Where the slopes begin to run in towards the Herive Burn, the route turns northwards and descends into the burn valley, which in spring is richly clothed in primroses. It crosses the burn by a sturdy footbridge and then weaves a mazy way through the trees, with views across to the hills on the south of the glen.

The Way drops down to the railway, passing an attractive waterfall, and then under a viaduct, and follows the south side of the A82 road for a short distance before crossing it, then sidles down a pathway below the road embankment and across a grassy meadow to the Kirkton bridge on the wide-flowing Fillan, a splendid viewpoint for the big Crianlarich hills; it then follows the farm road to Kirkton, and skirts the farm buildings on the left. The two farms on this side of the river are experimental units operated by the Scottish Agricultural College for the Department of Agriculture, so you are particularly requested not to take dogs on this part of the Way. If you do have a dog, you can skirt this section by following the main road till the Way crosses it again, about 1.25 km further west.

Among the trees by Kirkton Farm are the ruined remains of St Fillan's Chapel. An interpretive board tells something of the fascinating history of the man and his life. St Fillan was an Irish monk, the son of St Kentigerna who, as mentioned earlier, died on Inchcailloch in Loch Lomond in 734: he was active as a missionary in Breadalbane during the eighth century, and many miraculous tales of his exemplary life and work have been handed down. It is uncertain whether Fillan himself had a chapel here, but the site appears to have been a monastic establishment around the 12th century. It was raised to a priory by Robert the Bruce in 1318, and thereafter enjoyed some measure of privilege and protection from the Kings of Scotland.

The reasons for Bruce's particular beneficence can only be guessed at; he may well have received spiritual or secular assistance from the monks at the time of his defeat at nearby Dalrigh in 1306. According to one old tale, St Fillan gave a miraculous sign of his support to Bruce on the eve of the battle of Bannockburn. A relic of the saint, his arm-bone encased in silver, had been brought to the field as a talisman. As Bruce prayed before it, the case opened spontaneously to reveal the relic – to the astonishment of its priestly guardian, who (sensibly, in the circumstances) had brought only the case to Bannockburn, and had left the precious arm-bone in Strath Fillan for safety's sake.

The relics of St Fillan form perhaps the most remarkable part of the chapel's associations. Tradition relates that Fillan gave five symbols of his mission to lay brothers, who were required to act as custodians of the relics and to use them in appropriate circumstances, such as curing the sick or in the taking of oaths. These hereditary custodians, called in Gaelic *deoradh*, a stranger, anglicised as the surname Dewar, were given grants of land and special privileges which made them important dynasties in Glen Dochart and Strath Fillan; even the Reformation seems to have had little impact on their exalted status.

Only two of the relics are now known; the nature of the other three is a matter for speculation. The head of Fillan's crozier or staff, known as the Quigrich, travelled far with its keepers, and eventually went with them to Canada in

1818. By a series of happy coincidences it was recovered by the Society of Antiquaries of Scotland in 1877, and is now in the Museum of Scotland in Edinburgh. It is a superb piece of ornate silverwork, thought to be 14th century, but was found to contain within it a much older crozier of a severely simple design. St Fillan's bell is also in the Museum of Scotland after a rather similar career. It was stolen from the chapel by an English visitor in 1798, and retrieved only in 1869, through the good offices of the Bishop of Brechin.

The bell was kept at the chapel for use in a curious rite practised there as a supposed cure for insanity. Sufferers were dipped in a pool in the River Fillan known as the Holy Pool, carried to the chapel, and left overnight bound to a tombstone or the ancient font, with the bell over their head. In the morning it was expected that they would be found cured. The parish minister in 1843 took a wry view of these proceedings:

> 'We have not heard of any being cured; but the prospect of the ceremony, especially in a cold winter evening, might be a good test for persons pretending insanity.'

There are interpretive panels at the Chapel.

The Way follows the farm track along to the bridge at Auchtertyre Farm (which has no fewer than 16 wooden wigwams), and under a remarkable ridge of fluvio-glacial material back towards the river, which it reaches just above the Holy Pool. It crosses the A82 road at the north end of the new bridge across the Fillan, and continues along the river bank past the old White Bridge to the junction with the Crom Allt. A hundred metres or so up this burn a rough track crosses it on a sleeper bridge; at the top of the hill beyond, the West Highland Way turns sharp right on a grassy track which leads past a little lochan to a terrace edge above the Crom Allt. This terrace provides the line of the Way through the plantations up to the mature pinewood below Tyndrum.

The whole area around the River Cononish above White Bridge is a jumble of hummocky sands and gravels, partly terraced by river action and representing the finer material deposited by melt-water in the later stages of the last glaciation. This area is known as Dalrigh (the King's field),

Opposite: Keeping you on the right track.

commemorating a fight here in the summer of 1306 in which Robert the Bruce was defeated by the MacDougalls of Lome, allies of his arch-enemies the Comyns. Dalrigh marked the low point of Bruce's fortunes; after he had been crowned King of Scotland at Scone in March, and defeated at Methven, near Perth, by an English force in June, he had taken to the hills with a small company of supporters, only to meet defeat once more.

The exact location of the battle is unknown, but the general topography suggests that even with small forces it was more likely to be a running skirmish resulting from an ambush than a set-piece. Interestingly enough, Barbour in his epic poem *The Brus* described how the king fought off three attackers single-handed:

> '…in ane narow place
> Betuix ane lochside and ane bra
> That was so strat, I undirta,
> That he micht nocht wele turn his sted',

a description which fits the little lochan which the Way passes on the terrace above the Crom Allt.

From the terrace there is a good view over to the remnant pinewood of Coille Coire Chuilc above the Cononish backed by the broad slopes of Beinn Dubhchraig. This hill and its neighbours, Beinn Oss and Beinn Lui, make an excellent long day's walk by following up the Cononish track to the head of the glen. Lui, with its twin-topped ridge hanging above a steep north-eastern corrie bounded by craggy ribs, is by general consent one of the finest of Southern Highland hills, but it demands care, and should definitely not be tackled in snow conditions without appropriate equipment and experience in winter mountaineering.

At the lower edge of the pinewood just below Tyndrum a curious, barren patch of ground on the river bank is a reminder of a once thriving lead-mining industry carried on immediately to the south-west of Tyndrum and on the hills in the upper reaches of the Cononish River. The Tyndrum lead vein was discovered in 1741 while the mineral rights of the Breadalbane estates were on lease to Sir Robert Clifton, after whom the miners' village was named. Up to 1745 he extracted nearly 1700 tons of ore. Four successive companies then operated the mines, steadily till 1790 and intermittently thereafter till 1858, when the Marquis of Breadalbane resumed his rights and worked them till his death in 1862. Over that period of approximately a century another 5000 tons of ore were mined, much of it yielding lead at nearly 50% of the ore weight, as well as silver in very small quantities.

It was during the tenure of the Scots Mining Company from 1768 to 1790 that the crushing and smelting plant by the river was brought into operation; before then the crude ore was taken south by way of Loch Lomond at great expense. In its heyday the industry supported a population of around 200 in Clifton. In 1994 planning permission was given for gold to be extracted from a vein in Beinn Chuirn, north of Beinn Lui, but although preparatory work took place, extraction has never started.

The Way follows the Crom Allt burn, passing below the caravan site on the former goods yard by the station on the Oban railway line. It then goes through a wicket gate by the level crossing and across the gravel flats by the Crom Allt to the lower end of Clifton village, which is no more than a row of former miners' cottages. You will notice that the original axis of Clifton ran roughly south to north along the old road, but is now crossed at right angles by the main A82. There is a useful general store in the village – the last on the Way before Kinlochleven – as well as other shops, a restaurant and tearooms and hotel, bed and breakfast and bunkhouse accommodation, and a campsite. During the summer months there is also a tourist information service newly built in 1999. As at Crianlarich, there are bus and train services on all the routes through Tyndrum.

Tyndrum means simply 'the house of the ridge', the ridge in this case being the main east-west watershed of Scotland a short distance to the west. Perhaps because it stands far inland at the headwaters of the Tay, the inn at Tyndrum was long thought to be, as the Old Statistical Account put it in 1793, 'one of the highest inhabited situations in North Britain'. In fact it stands at around 230 metres, which is substantially lower than large settlements like Braemar or Wanlockhead.

Tyndrum was something of a service centre during the 18th and 19th centuries for the cattle droving trade, when the small black cattle of the Highlands were moved south

'on the hoof' to the markets or trysts at Crieff or Falkirk, where they were sold to Lowland or English dealers. Latterly there was a smithy where cattle could be shod – an unlikely but necessary measure when the beasts moved from the soft open ground of the upland drove routes to the enclosed gravel roads of the lower ground. There was a 'stance' where cattle and sheep could be rested overnight, and the inn, maintained by Lord Breadalbane, for the drovers themselves.

The intrepid Mrs Sarah Murray of Kensington put up at Tyndrum one wet autumn night in 1799 during her first tour in Scotland, just as the drovers were making their way home to the Highlands from Falkirk Tryst. As the evening wore on, the inn gradually filled to bursting point: 'this continued till the house was in a perfect up-roar: my servants could not get a place to put their heads in. My man took his sleep in the carriage: and the poor horses were almost crushed to death in the stables'.

Things are not so very different in Tyndrum in high summer nowadays, when the village is full of the bustle and traffic of a busy tourist centre. In the winter or in wet weather, however, it can still be as Queen Victoria saw it when she passed through in 1875, 'a wild, picturesque and desolate spot'. A little later, the railway that brought the Queen to Tyndrum also made it a popular venue for the climbing meets of the newly-founded Scottish Moun-taineering Club, as recorded in the deathless doggerel of the Club Song:

> '...the best of the Club will then be afoot,
> From the President down to the last recruit,
> And a merry band you'll find us,
> As we leave the town behind us,
> When we go up to the mountains in the snow.

> You may tell Tyndrum that we're going to come,
> And at snug Dalmally will our hillmen rally,
> And a lot of other places
> Will behold our jolly faces,
> When we go up to the mountains in the snow.'

J. G. Stott, the man who wrote these lines, emigrated to New Zealand shortly afterwards and helped found the New Zealand Alpine Club.

Opposite: The unmistakable shape of Beinn Dorain.

Tyndrum – Bridge of Orchy
(11 km; 6.75 miles)

FROM the upper end of Clifton village the Way climbs by the burnside towards the pass ahead in a purposeful manner which indicates that it is once more back on the line of the old military road. In fact, the Way makes use of the old road for much of the rest of its length, and diverges from it only slightly until within about 7 km of Fort William, when it breaks away to cross into Glen Nevis. Most of this distance gives excellent walking on a very clear track.

The first section, as far as Bridge of Orchy, is around 10 km long. This part of the Caulfeild road network was constructed by troops drawn from Rich's Regiment and the Buffs between 1750 and 1752 and was later adopted as the line of the old main road north through Glen Coe. The new road, built in the late 1920s and early '30s, takes a sweeping curve westwards from Clifton past its junction with the Oban road, returning to join up with the old road and the railway as they enter the defile through to Glen Orchy. As it was built on a completely new line over much of its length, the new road is characterised by long, even curves and easy gradients. Although it is now taken very much for granted, at the time of its building amenity and recreation interests objected very strongly to its effect on the landscape, describing it as a 'million-pound racetrack'. The tall snowposts along the roadsides are useful not so much in deep snow, for the road is well serviced by snowploughs, so that it is rarely blocked in winter, but in conditions of general snow cover and poor visibility.

As the Way climbs the hill there are fine views back across the head of Strath Fillan to the bulk of Beinn Dubhchraig and over the workings and debris of the lead mines on Sron nan Colan behind Clifton. The workings cover a very restricted area on a single main vein associated with an almost vertical fault line, which has been picked out by erosion. In fact the quartz 'mother vein' continues northwards in the glen of the Crom Allt beside the Way, and it may be possible to detect the signs of excavation where unprofitable exploratory pits were dug around the stream. It is well worth examining the little gorge of the Crom Allt for its own sake, for it has one or two fine miniature cascades and 'punchbowls'; but the upper part of the little glen is now dominated by the storage tanks and treatment plant of Tyndrum's water supply.

The steep-sided pass through to Glen Orchy is most probably another product of the last glacial epoch, when great glaciers flowed southwards from the major centre of ice accumulation on Rannoch Moor, and over-rode the cols on ridges to the south. The slopes of Beinn Odhar on the right have been over-steepened in the process; the conspicuous scree-fans from the little burns on this flank, and the very clear terracettes or sheeptracks, testify to the slope's gradual adjustment under the force of gravity. It is not surprising that the soldiers building the military road spent much time and effort in this area clearing the road after rainstorms and spring thaws.

On the long, gradual ascent to the summit of the pass, Beinn Dubhchraig, a feature of the view from Rowchoish Bothy onwards, passes gradually out of sight to the rear, just as the next of the great mountain mileposts of the West Highland Way, Beinn Dorain, soars into view ahead. With its bald, bouldery pate, sweeping slope to westward, and gully-seamed flanks, Dorain is a distinctive and challenging peak if not, perhaps, a very beautiful one. It dominates the Way as it passes the local authority boundary on the summit, leaving Stirling for Argyll and Bute, and also finally leaving the National Park. The path traverses above the east side of the railway line for 300 metres or so before descending sharply to a sheep-creep which allows passage through under the line to rejoin the old road. A little further down, the little schisty crags above the road are veritable hanging gardens of the yellow mountain saxifrage in summer.

The full, thousand-metre bulk of Beinn Dorain becomes ever more evident on the descent into Auch Gleann, where the wide horizontals of the open valley floor seem to sharpen the mountain's vertical contrast. The railway's remarkable horseshoe curve under the flanks of Beinn Odhar, Beinn a'Chaisteil and Beinn Dorain, and its viaducts over the intervening glens, lend further emphasis to the scale and steepness of the peaks.

Although these hills are now given over mainly to sheep-grazing, and increasingly to forestry, they were in medieval times a hunting preserve, part of the royal deer forest of Mamlorn. The term 'forest', though traditional, is misleading, for most deer forests are largely, if not totally, devoid of trees. The deer forests in this area in the seventeenth century are listed by an unknown topographer in Macfarlane's Geographical Collections:

> 'first is Coryba in Bra-glen-crevirne (this is Coire Ba in the Black Mount, which the Way passes on Rannoch Moor). Item Maim, Laerne is the kings forrest very riche in deer, lying upon Brae-Wrchay (Orchy). Brae-Lyon, and Brae-Lochy 10 myl of lenth. Item Bin Dowran a forest in Bra-Glen-Wrchay 5 myl long.'

Auch - the name is short for *Ach-innis-chalean*, the field of the hazel meadow - was once a royal hunting lodge, and it is known that James IV visited it for a week during the autumn of 1506. The Campbells of Glenorchy, the hereditary keepers of the forest, and the forebears of the Earls of Breadalbane, were required to supply venison to the king, particularly for royal feasts; venison was even salted and exported to Spain.

The deer forests also served as inspiration for one of Gaeldom's greatest poets, Duncan Ban Macintyre, who was a stalker in Mamlorn. *Donnchadh Ban nan Oran* (fair-haired Duncan the poet - literally 'of the songs') was born near Loch Tulla in 1724, and although the details of his life are uncertain, he is believed to have lived for several years at Ais-an t-Sithein in Gleann Chonoghlais behind Beinn Dorain. Unsympathetic commentators suggest that Duncan Ban took to poetry in self-justification after the 1745 Jacobite Rising. He was called out in the Argyll Militia on the Hanoverian side, and participated very briefly in the Battle of Falkirk in January 1746, where he was one of the first to turn and run when the Jacobite clansmen charged. However, since it is thought that Duncan had no very strong loyalties to either side, but had been sent as a substitute for one of his feudal superiors, Fletcher of Crannach, we can have some sympathy for him. In later life he left Glen Orchy for

Opposite: Crossing the railway outside Tyndrum.

Edinburgh and became an officer of the City Guard - effectively a policeman - before dying there in 1812.

Although Macintyre was illiterate, he was well aware of the works of other Gaelic poets, and friends transcribed his compositions for him. His own best poems are full of enthusiasm for the mountains, the deer, and the chase, but they were composed for singing or recitation, and do not fare well in translation. His long poem in praise of Beinn Dorain is generally considered to be his masterpiece, but a verse or two from his Final Farewell to the Bens (*Cead Deireannach nam Beann*) demonstrate an enthusiasm which walkers on the Way will share:

> I was on Ben Dobhrain yesterday,
> no stranger in her bounds was I;
> I looked upon the glens
> and the bens that I had known so well;
> this was a happy picture—
> to be tramping on the hillsides,
> at the hour the sun was rising,
> and the deer would be a-bellowing.
> Blithely would I set out
> for stalking on the hill passes
> away to climb rough country,
> and late would I be coming home;
> the clean rain and the air
> on the peaks of the high mountains,
> helped me to grow, and gave me
> robustness and vitality.
> Farewell to the deer forests—
> O! they are wondrous hill-country,
> with green cress and spring water,
> a noble, royal, pleasant drink;
> to the moor plains which are well beloved,
> and the pastures which are plentiful,
> as these are parts of which I've taken leave,
> my thousand blessings aye be theirs.
> (from *The Songs of Duncan Ban Macintyre,* edited by
> Angus MacLeod, Edinburgh 1952).

The Way crosses the Allt Chonoghlais at Auch by an old bridge of great character, kept in use by the Army's practical, if incongruous, repairs to its northern span.

Beinn Dorain looms steeply above, and a way can readily be found round the broken crags to its top. However, it may not be so easy to find a route downwards, particularly in mist, and Bridge of Orchy is probably a better starting-point for the ascent, since what that approach lacks in drama it makes up for in easier gradient.

Continuing on the old road, the West Highland Way turns left along the river flats and contours on a slightly rising line across the foot of Dorain's great parabolic slope, beneath its runnels and gullies, to cross the railway, now returned from its long horseshoe bend to the east. This section of the Way gives pleasant, easy walking, looking down over the wide glen where the river winds gently north between alder-lined banks to join the Orchy, and forward to where Stob Ghabhar and its mountain peers in the Blackmount ranges begin to take their place as the next milestone.

Closer to Bridge of Orchy there are long views southwestwards down Glen Orchy, with in certain lights a singular feature in the long, upstanding quartzite dyke on the north spur of Beinn Udlaidh. Nearer at hand, the massive boulder of Clach a'Bhein may well have fallen from Beinn Dorain to come to rest amidst the moraine on the valley floor. Rightwards, the wild and rough Coire an Dothaidh divides Beinn Dorain from its sister peak of Dothaidh on the north.

Hereabouts the railway line runs down steady gradients towards Bridge of Orchy, which is the lowest point before it begins its 37 km climb round the eastern edge of Rannoch Moor to its summit at 411 metres beyond Corrour Station. Thereby hangs a tale related by John Thomas in his history, *The West Highland Railway*, concerning the misadventures of a guard on the early morning freight train from Glasgow to Fort William. The story goes that the guard was sound asleep in his brake van at the rear when his driver's sharp opening of the throttle as the engine crossed the Corrour Summit broke the coupling of the van - which set off downhill, backwards, with its sleeping occupant. The signalmen along the line, loath to derail the runaway van with the guard aboard, let it run past at speeds of up to 55 kmph. At last the van came to a halt on these rising grades south of Bridge of Orchy, where the stationmaster found the guard still fast asleep - and back to where he had been two hours before, having rolled back a distance of 40 km!

The Way enters Bridge of Orchy by the underpass at the station. The village, scattered along the axis of the old road between the station and the bridge, is one of those Highland settlements which appear on the map to be a major centre, but on closer acquaintance turn out to be a few houses and a hotel in the midst of largely uninhabited and empty country. You can stop in Bridge of Orchy at the hotel, which has a bunkhouse for those seeking lower cost accommodation (although at present without self-catering facilities). There are both bus and train services northwards to Fort William and southwards towards Glasgow. Anyone wanting to camp should enquire at the hotel, as some of the land is owned by Forest Enterprise, who have a strict No Camping policy. Intending campers should note that the average annual rainfall recorded here between 1864 and 1873 was 3000 mm, and that similar levels can be expected from here on northwards, at least among the hills.

By dint of its strategic location on the southern fringes of Rannoch Moor, Bridge of Orchy has a role in two of the historical novels of Neil Munro, *John Splendid* and *The New Road,* in both of which the heroes make long and adventurous journeys northwards from the Campbell lands in Argyll into the central Highlands. In *John Splendid* the Bridge of Orchy itself is the scene for a missed rendezvous and a cryptic message. The hero's confederates had left on the parapet: 'three sprigs of gall, a leaf of ivy . . . and a bare twig of oak standing up at a slant . . . held down by a peeled willow withy, one end of which pointed in the direction of the glen'. These mystic symbols were interpreted to mean that three Campbells, a Stewart and a Gordon had gone hurrying south down Glen Orchy at 3pm the previous day! In *The New Road,* Aeneas Macmaster stops the night in the inn at Bridge of Orchy before crossing the Moor to Kingshouse by a devious mountain route to evade pursuit. The inn is described as: 'shabby to the point of scandal, no better than a common tavern, smokeblackened, smelling of the reek of peat and mordants used in dyeing cloth; lit by cruisies, going like a fair with traffic', the traffic being mainly cattle drovers.

Both are excellent stories well told, but reflect more credit on Munro's lively imagination than on his historical research. The tale of *John Splendid* is woven into the history of the Marquis of Montrose's campaign against Argyll in 1645, about a century before there is any record of a bridge at Bridge of Orchy; and *The New Road* is set in about 1730, when there is no record of an inn, or indeed of any habitation at all, where Bridge of Orchy now stands. But these considerations should deter no-one from reading the novels, which not only evoke the landscape of the country around the Way, but also give a vivid sense of the tensions and insecurity of life in the Highlands of three centuries ago.

Bridge of Orchy Hotel.

Bridge of Orchy.

Bridge of Orchy – Kingshouse

SUMMARY

Distance: 19km (12 miles).

Height Range: 150-350m.

Terrain: From Bridge of Orchy to Victoria Bridge is straight-forward, with one moderate climb. After Victoria Bridge the route follows the old road (good walking surface) across the western edge of Rannoch Moor, rising to 350m and very exposed in bad weather with no shelter of any kind until White Corries ski area is reached. Magnificent scenery but in poor conditions a tough stage.

Opposite: Looking back to Bridge of Orchy.

Rannoch Moor

IT is impossible to set precise limits to Rannoch Moor, because a moor is in one sense a subjective experience rather than simply a geographical feature. But Rannoch Moor is usually taken as centring on the large triangular plateau bounded on the west by the Black Mount hills, on the south and east by Loch Tulla and the range from Beinn an Dothaidh to Beinn a'Chreachain, and on the north by the high ground from Beinn a'Chrulaiste to A'Chruach above Loch Laidon. The West Highland Way thus skirts only the western fringe of the Moor, but it does capture a good deal of the character of the place.

It may be debatable whether Rannoch is the biggest or bleakest of Scottish moors, but few would deny that it is the grandest. Its fringing frieze of mountains, its irregular knolls and ridges, and its spidery tracery of lochs and rivers lend variety without diminishing its sternness. Geologically, the moor is described as a 'great granodiorite batholith', a relatively uniform mass of medium-grained grey granite, thought to be of Lower Old Red Sandstone age - about 400 million years old. Its present form as a chaotically ill-drained, bog-blanketed basin results from its role as a great gathering-ground of ice during the last glaciation, combined with the effects of high rainfall and extreme exposure.

Despite its inhospitability and barrenness, Rannoch Moor has played its part in the human history of the Highlands. Its strategic location astride the main inland route northwards to Lochaber has led to a steady stream of traffic, military and civil, over the centuries: the old tag 'that thorofare of thieves' is only part of the picture. The story of the evolving lines of communication and their construction across the Moor is a romantic one in itself, while the hostelries on and around the Moor - Hobson's Choice for accommodation in an empty land - are well-known through travellers' tales.

The impression that the Moor creates will depend very much on the visitor's attitude and on the circumstances of weather and season: writers as various as Thomas Pennant and T. S. Eliot have been moved to record their reactions in prose and verse. In fine weather, with the lark overhead and the bog cotton snowy-white by tiny, calm pools that reflect the blue of the wide sky, the Moor belies its reputation as a desolate wilderness. In rain or snow with low cloud driving before a gale, it tends to promote the conviction that Hell need not be hot.

Bridge of Orchy — Inveroran
(4 km; 2.5 miles)

AT Bridge of Orchy, the West Highland Way leaves the railway and the road which it has paralleled since Glen Falloch. It does not meet the railway again till Fort William, and the road not till Kingshouse, 18 km to the north. The first stage of the journey over Rannoch Moor is an introductory, short leg to the Inveroran Hotel by Loch Tulla.

The Way sets off westwards from the crossroads over the old bridge, beneath which the Orchy, sprawling or brawling according to the weather, runs southwards over its bed of great rock slabs. The river must have represented a formidable obstacle to travellers before the bridge was built by the military in about 1751. According to General Roy's Military Survey, carried out at about the same time as Caulfeild's road-building programme in this area, the track over Rannoch Moor prior to the military road did not cross the Orchy at all; it ran north to Achallader, forded the Water of Tulla, and ascended the Black Mount on a line close to the present main road before striking westwards under Meall Beag to the route of the old Glen Coe road.

A few metres beyond the bridge, the Way deserts the old Glen Coe road, which holds to the flats along Loch Tulla side, and strikes up through the forestry plantations on the military road, which here as elsewhere takes the direct route over the hill in preference to a detour on the flat. This stretch over the Mam Carraigh was built around 1752-53, and has been less altered from its original state than most of the military road, for it seems to have been abandoned for the longer but lower route round the lochshore at an early date. When William and Dorothy Wordsworth came this way from Glen Coe in 1803, it is clear from Dorothy's journal that they followed a road around the shore of Loch Tulla.

The going on the old road is inclined to be rather wet, as it climbs gradually rightwards through the plantations, before traversing back and onwards again to a cairn at the highest point, 320 metres, on the ridge of Ben Inverveigh. In good weather this is one of the Way's most dramatic viewpoints. The whole range of the Blackmount Forest is spread out to the west and north, 'a wild tangle of long ridges and deep corries, with bold granite peaks and craggy outcrops', as W. H. Murray describes it. There is excellent hill-walking on and among these mountains, which have a distinct but indefinable atmosphere of their own.

To the north-east the bleak sweep of Rannoch Moor leads round to the rampart of massive hills from Beinn a'Chreachain, by Achaladair and Dothaidh to Dorain, and thence southwards to where the wide flats of Auch Gleann rise into the window of the pass through to Tyndrum. Behind, a well-built stalkers' track climbs the long slope of Ben Inverveigh. In the foreground below, Loch Tulla lies under the moor, with a dark scarf of woodland round its shores sheltering the Victorian lodge of Black Mount. The islet of Eilean Stalcair, with its few pines, appears to have been at least in part artificial, built up with timber and stone, though there are no evident signs of human habitation; it may have been simply a place of refuge.

Under Mam Carraigh the magnificent pine woods that run down to the loch, the Doire Darach, represent another remnant of the ancient Caledonian pine forest. This particular wood has a special interest for ecologists, as the Marchioness of Breadalbane had some of it fenced about 100 years ago, to exclude deer and so encourage the regeneration of the pines. The whole wood conveys a sense of ecological vitality that is quite absent among the scattered, moribund pines of the upper part of Glen Falloch.

It is not generally realised that the Loch Tulla area can boast 'parallel roads' similar to the well-known features of Glen Roy, though these are less well defined. In certain conditions of light and vegetation growth, you may be able to trace as many as five terraces on the slopes either

Opposite: Looking down on Loch Tulla.

side of the valley of the Water of Tulla above Achallader farm. These ancient lake-shores were formed in the last glacial period when a lobe of ice from Rannoch Moor choked the drainage of the upper valley. As the ice gradually wasted away, it allowed the dammed-up waters to escape westwards by a succession of channels at progressively lower levels.

From its summit, the military road runs gently down towards Inveroran, giving a good forward prospect of the next section of the Way round the head of the loch and up onto the moor. The little hotel at Inveroran stands hard by the bridge on the Allt Orain. Facing east and close-sheltered by trees, it appears the very epitome of a snug haven in the wild country around. There has been an inn here for over two centuries; and standing as it does almost alone in the midst of an empty tract of mountain and moor, it has gathered its full share of historical and literary anecdote.

Just two or three kilometres to the west, in a croft called Druimlaighart above the Allt Tolaghan, Duncan Ban Macintyre was born. As we have already seen, he did not move far beyond Glen Orchy before his eventual final migration to Edinburgh, and it is thus not surprising to find that he married the daughter of the Inveroran innkeeper, Mary, and immortalised her in another of his songs.

The Wordsworths took breakfast at the inn during their tour of 1803, and though they were made very welcome, found the fare less than appetising: 'the butter not eatable, the barley-cakes fusty, the oat-bread so hard I could not chew it, and there were only four eggs in the house, which they had boiled hard as stones'. Nevertheless Dorothy observed with characteristic sympathy the scene in the kitchen, where:

> 'about seven or eight travellers, probably drovers, with as many dogs, were sitting in a complete circle round a large peat-fire in the middle of the floor, each with a mess of porridge, in a wooden vessel, upon his knee; a pot, suspended from one of the black beams, was boiling on the fire; two or three women pursuing their household business on the outside of the circle, children playing on the floor.

There was nothing uncomfortable in this confusion: happy, busy, or vacant faces, all looked pleasant; and even the smoky air, being a sort of natural indoor atmosphere of Scotland, served only to give a softening, I may say harmony, to the whole'.

Sixteen years later, when Robert Southey came past on his own travels with Thomas Telford, he thought the inn was a 'wretched hovel', but noted that Lord Breadalbane was building a new one.

Like the other old inns along the Way, at Inverarnan, Tyndrum and Kingshouse, Inveroran probably derived most of its trade from the droving traffic. There was a stance here, where the drovers could rest their beasts overnight and find grazing for them. In his classic account *The Drove Roads of Scotland*, A. R. B. Haldane tells us that something like 70,000 sheep and 8-10,000 cattle moved south by this route every year, and that the traditional grazing fees were 1/6d (7 1/2 new pence) for 20 cattle or 100 sheep. These facts emerged from a notable lawsuit brought by drovers against Lord Breadalbane, who in 1844 proposed to close the traditional stance in order to preserve his land for deer stalking. Breadalbane finally won the case on appeal to the House of Lords and the stance was removed to Bridge of Orchy. It is interesting to note that the drover named in the lawsuit as chief pursuer against the landowner was a MacGregor . . .

Inveroran also has an honoured place in the history of Scottish mountaineering, for the inn was the base of some of the earliest meets of the SMC in the 1890s. Indeed, it can claim to be one of the cradles of the Scottish tradition of snow and ice climbing, for the pioneers tackled some of their first winter routes in and around the icy Upper Couloir of Stob Ghabhar, the closest of the high Blackmount peaks.

The Easter Meet of 1892 was also the occasion of a notable walking feat by two of the founders of the club, W. W. Naismith and Gilbert Thomson. These two took a night train from Glasgow to Dalwhinnie, at the head of Strath Spey, arriving at 3.30am. They walked down the shores of Loch Ericht, over the great plateau of Ben Alder, and across the full extent of Rannoch Moor, to join the Meet at Inveroran at 8pm. This jaunt of over 65 km, with

a good deal of climbing thrown in, seems to have caused them no particular exertion, and both were out on the hills with their clubmates the next day.

The hotel now offers accommodation, meals and all modern comforts. Permission should be sought from the hotel by anyone wishing to camp in the area. Tracks lead westwards towards the superb hills overlooking Glen Etive, with Ben Starav the prince among them. A splendid low-level walk goes down Glen Kinglass to Taynuilt. On the way you pass a climbing hut at Clashgour, about 2km west of Forest Lodge. The hut, a compact corrugated iron shed, was once the school attended by children from Clashgour and the few dwellings round Loch Tulla. It is legendary among the Scottish climbing fraternity for nights of phenomenal overcrowding, because although the hut has the rough dimensions of an oversize sentry-box and comfortably sleeps six, it is claimed that the all-time record of bodies spending the night inside (it seems fatuous to talk of sleeping) is 35. The Black Hole of Calcutta must have been pleasant by comparison.

Inveroran — Kingshouse
(15.25 km; 9.5 miles)

FROM Inveroran the Way rounds the flats at the head of Loch Tulla, climbs on to the Blackmount, and skirts the western edge of Rannoch Moor under the flanks of the massive mountains that enclose Coire Ba. This stage has a natural unity: it was a day's journey for the old drovers, from one stance at Kingshouse to another at Inveroran. It is potentially the most serious stretch of the West Highland Way, for while there is an excellent track over the whole distance, it runs at a high level, is very exposed and virtually without any shelter for over 10 km, and offers no easy retreat in foul weather. In such conditions the choice is merely between pressing on and returning by the same route. It should be borne in mind that the western edge of the Moor has an average annual rainfall in the region of 3000 mm.

Opposite: Lochan na h-Achlaise, Rannoch Moor.

For the fit and experienced hill-walker, a superb alternative route is available outside the deer-stalking season (which runs from mid-August to mid-October). The high level traverse to Kingshouse over Stob Ghabhar and Clach Leathad is a classic ridge walk involving some 18 km of walking and around 1400 metres of ascent, depending on the number of tops taken in. The SMC Guide *The Central Highlands* should be consulted for further details, and the route should definitely not be tackled without the appropriate skills and equipment; the route-finding is not altogether straightforward, and can be difficult in mist.

From Inveroran the Way starts gently, winding first west then north towards Victoria Bridge and Forest Lodge. In winter and early spring red deer can frequently be seen on the flats. Forest Lodge, set in a pine plantation, is a typical Victorian 'shooting box' with a hint of the Black Forest in its architecture, a product of the great deer-stalking industry that dominated much of the Highlands in the 19th century, reaching its zenith in the 30 or 40 years before the First World War. At that time the Blackmount forest and all the ground over to Loch Etive was owned by the third Marquis of Breadalbane, whose favourite recreation was deerstalking. His wife too was a keen stalker, and her account of stalking days around the turn of the century, *The High Tops of Black Mount*, is well worth reading. It is an unpretentious record of long hard days on the mountains in pursuit of the stag, and whatever one's attitude to the hunt, the Marchioness's sheer enthusiasm for mountain and corrie, and her enormous relish of the physical toil and satisfaction of hill days, are irresistible.

Appropriately, when the Ladies' Scottish Climbing Club was formed in 1908, the Marchioness was chosen to be the club's first Honorary President. Her later life was less happy; after the Marquis's death in 1922 she retired to Ardmaddy Castle in Nether Lorn and died there ten years later. Before her death the Breadalbane Trustees were forced to sell off her beloved Blackmount and other huge tracts of the estates in order to pay death duties.

The military road heads straight up the hill behind Forest Lodge, but the Way holds to the old Glen Coe road on a lower line, climbing gradually rightwards above the woods behind Black Mount Lodge. The origin of the name

'Blackmount' for this area is uncertain, though it may well have referred to the peat hags on the moor. In the Highlands 'mount', or 'mounth', usually implies not a hill as such, but a high plateau, often with a pass across it. In this sense the title of Blackmount has been current since at least the late 18th century. The transference to include the deer forest and mountain range to the west seems to be more recent.

As the track climbs steadily towards its first summit on the moor, at around 320 metres, it gives a wide outlook over Loch Tulla to the Achaladair hills, but the focus of interest changes when the Way turns northwards. At the moorland summit between Meall Beag and Beinn Toaig you cross from Argyll and Bute into Highland for the remainder of the route; and from the Orchy drainage, flowing to the Atlantic, back into the Tay system. Attention now centres on the vast, wild recess of Coire Ba to the west of the road, and on the great mountains that form its walls and throw down craggy ridges to its wide, peat-hagged floor. It is not difficult to imagine great glaciers pouring down from the corries under Stob Ghabhar and Clach Leathad to augment the huge ice field that lay over the moor not so many thousand years ago.

In summer even this wild scene has its charming points of detail. The drier knolls are clad in purple heather, the damp hollows in strong-scented myrtle; the wet flats are dotted with the snowy plumes of bog cotton and the golden-yellow spikes of bog asphodel, with the delicate pinkish-purple of the heath spotted orchid here and there. Wherever the underlying peat is exposed, bleached and gnarled remnants of pine roots may be seen within it. These former pinewoods, once extensive, may have suffered the same fate as other parts of the Old Wood of Caledon - reduction by cutting, burning, and grazing - but climatic factors may also have played a substantial part in their demise on this high, wet and particularly exposed site.

Ba Bridge is perhaps the remotest part of the West Highland Way. The River Ba forces its way eastwards through a rocky gut and descends to wind across a wide boggy flat; to the west, rough ridges rise to high peaks. Coire Ba has always been a haunt of the red deer, and around the month of October, with the wind in the right

quarter, you may hear the corrie resound to the calling of red deer stags in the rut. It is not a beautiful noise - a long, low, aggressive, throaty braying; but it has immense power to evoke the atmosphere of wild hills and open moor.

Coire Ba and its deer are the basis of a well-known story dating back to the time of James VI and I. In 1621 the King heard that a white hind, presumably a rare albino, had been sighted in Coire Ba, and despatched one of his servants, John Scandoner, to capture it alive. Unfortunately Scandoner arrived in the area in February 1622 and met the kind of weather that might be expected in Coire Ba at that season. He did sight the white hind, but despite the aid of a company of men lent by Sir Duncan Campbell of Glenorchy, he failed to catch it. The King then sent the hapless Scandoner to Glen Artney in Perthshire, apparently to practise on ordinary red deer before returning to the pursuit of the white hind; but he seems never to have come back to Coire Ba. Looking at the ground it is easy to appreciate the difficulties he faced.

From Ba Bridge the Way climbs again, past the remains of Ba Cottage and the junction with a track leading down to the A82 road, which can be seen a few kilometres to the east, tracing a route between the large lochans on the flattest part of the moor. This summit is the highest point on the West Highland Way so far, at about 450 metres. Not far above this point, and visible for some distance from the southern approach, is a small cairn, a simple memorial to Peter Fleming, who died of a heart attack while shooting over the Blackmount forest on 18 August 1971. Fleming was a most remarkable man whose career was full of incidents no less colourful and dramatic than those inflicted on James Bond by his novelist brother, Ian Fleming. Among his travels, many of them as a special correspondent for *The Times,* he took part in an abortive expedition to the Amazon jungle in search of the long-lost Colonel Fawcett, and roamed widely through Central Asia. In World War Two, Fleming of necessity became a specialist in escaping from occupied countries, and he did so successively from Norway, Greece and Burma.

Opposite: Ba Bridge and the River Ba.
Overleaf: Blackrock Cottage and Buachaille Etive Mor.

The memorial commands a superb panorama of the Moor, though the outlook might be characterised as 'Caledonia stern and wild', since it consists almost exclusively of mountain, moor and lochan, with not more than two or three human habitations in sight. Eastwards, the Moor stretches away in a patternless mosaic of lochans and pools, hummocks and boulders, boggy flats and bare hills: in Principal Shairp's terms:

'…a desert wide and wasted,
Washed by rain-floods to the bones;
League on league of heather blasted,
Storm-gashed moss, grey boulder-stones.'

From this bleak splendour the eye lifts to the encircling ranges. Many of the tops to the south will by this stage be old friends to walkers doing the whole Way, but you may be able to pick out one or two new peaks in Mamlorn and the Loch Rannoch area. Just to the south of the dip in the skyline through by Strath Tummel, Schiehallion may be visible as a slightly lop-sided pyramid. The isolation and simple form of this mountain made it the subject of a four-months scientific programme in 1774, when the Astronomer Royal of the time, Nevil Maskelyne, used the peak to calculate the mass of the earth. To the northeast the huge plateau of Ben Alder may be seen, while the eastern tops of the Grey Corries range and the hills around Loch Treig appear over Black Corries Lodge to the north.

This extravaganza of mountain scenery continues as the Way follows the old road, here rather rough and broken in places, round the flanks of Meall a'Bhuiridh to descend gently into the wide basis that drains to the River Etive. Far ahead in the portals of Glen Coe you may spy the plantation at Altnafeadh, marking the foot of the Devil's Staircase track, by which the Way climbs over to Kinlochleven. To its left there gradually appears the dramatic and craggy bastion of Stob Dearg of Buachaille Etive Mor, 'the great herdsman of Etive', perhaps the finest of the Way's mountain mileposts. Like a neolithic arrowhead, in W. H. Murray's telling phrase, it dominates the whole of this part of the Way.

Closer at hand on the left, under Meall a'Bhuiridh, are the chairlift and other facilities of the White Corries ski centre. The lift goes up to ski runs on the upper slopes beneath the summit of the mountain, above 750 metres. The skiing potential of Meall a'Bhuiridh was first explored by a party from the Ladies' Scottish Climbing Club in 1917. In the mid 1950s a tow was set up and in 1960 the chairlift was built by Scotland's first commercial skifield company, White Corries Ltd.

Skiing at Glencoe — as the area became popularly known — was never on the large scale of Cairngorm, Glen Shee or Aonach Mor (Nevis Range) beyond Fort William, partly because of the lack of nearby accommodation. However, it had a regular weekend clientele, particularly from the Glasgow area, and the runs on Meall a'Bhuiridh were renowned for their variety and quality. The ski area closed in November 2003, due to the lack of regular snow, with no plans at that time for a reopening.

The Way joins the tarmac road up to the ski car park just opposite Blackrock Cottage, run by the LSCC and available to members of kindred clubs. Blackrock is a small, snug hut of great charm, with a unique and almost tangible atmosphere derived from its lonely position. No-one who has the good fortune to stay there on a clear autumn or winter night, when the silent moor and stark peaks lie under a bowl of stars, will readily forget the experience.

From Blackrock the Way swings downhill over the moor, crosses the main road which it last met at Bridge of Orchy, and descends towards Kingshouse Hotel, nestling among pines in a wide hollow under the great, bare whaleback of Beinn a'Chrulaiste. As the perspective changes on Buachaille Etive Mor, you will see that Stob Dearg is not an individual rock peak, but the craggy northern end of a range of ragged hills stretching down Glen Etive. To complement it on the other side of the glen, the broken ridge of Sron na Creise emerges from behind Creag Dhubh of Meall a'Bhuiridh. Kingshouse is thus framed in one of the noblest settings of mountain and moor that Scotland can show.

Although Kingshouse Hotel has been completely modernised, it was evidently a going concern 200 years ago — not, perhaps, a long history by lowland standards, but remarkable for an inn in such a remote and uninhabited location. Indeed, the problems of running the inn

were acknowledged by the Government, who for long contributed an annual grant to keep it open, and charged no rent. Nevertheless, the accounts of early tourists make it clear that the management of the inn left a great deal to be desired: in 1803 Dorothy Wordsworth, usually very tolerant of primitive accommodation, was forthright in her condemnation: 'Never did I see such a miserable, such a wretched place'.

The shortcomings in management in those days may be explained by the concern of successive innkeepers with the business of salt-smuggling, a trade in which Kingshouse seems to have played an important part. To modern ears, salt sounds an unlikely contraband, but at the end of the 18th century it was subject to a heavy duty - except where it was to be used to preserve fish for export: and that was the salt which was trafficked. Southey records that one innkeeper at Kingshouse made enough from salt in ten years to buy a farm and retire on the proceeds: 'the excise officers give very little interruption to this trade, because the value of a seizure is far from being an adequate compensation for the trouble and risque of making it'.

The smuggling of salt, however, can hardly be blamed for conditions at Kingshouse in the 1920s, when J.H.B. Bell, one of the great names of Scottish mountaineering, used the inn as a base. 'From one's bedroom' he declared, 'one could smell the bacon frying through a hole in the floor, which was better than a breakfast gong. In another room, it was said to be necessary to put up an umbrella in bed if the weather was wet, which was very often the case'.

Happily, all this is in the past, and the hotel now boasts all the modern amenities. It is the only accommodation available, although a fuller range of services and accommodation can be found in and around Glencoe village, some 19 km to the west, and the Glasgow to Fort William bus service on the A82 road provides a means of getting there.

Opposite: Approaching Kingshouse after the crossing of Rannoch Moor.

Snow and frost enhance the beauty of Buachaille Etive Mor, near Kingshouse.

Kingshouse – Kinlochleven

SUMMARY

Distance: 14.5 km (9 miles).

Height Range: 250-500-50m.

Terrain: From Kingshouse the Way enters the sublime scenery of Glencoe and at Altnafeadh climbs over the Devil's Staircase, an old military road, to its highest point at nearly 500m before a long descent into Kinlochleven. Paths and good tracks but, although short, still a hard stage in bad weather. Glorious mountain views throughout.

Opposite: Glencoe from the Devil's Staircase.

THE West Highland Way continues to follow the old military road as it runs westwards towards the head of Glen Coe, before climbing sharply northwards up the bounding wall of Rannoch Moor to the highest point on the Way, the top of the Devil's Staircase at 550 metres. From there the old road and the Way descend gently, contouring round the northern spurs of the Aonach Eagach ridge, until they make a final plunge to sea level at Kinlochleven. In clear weather this stretch offers magnificent mountain views, first of the dramatic and rugged peaks around the head of Glen Coe and Glen Etive, and later of the great ranges between Loch Leven and Ben Nevis.

In bad weather it is potentially dangerous; there is no shelter at all on the exposed upper part of the Way between Altnafeadh and the buildings at the head of the Kinlochleven pipeline race (GR 202604) — not so much as a tree or a standing wall. While the Way is evident on the ground in fair weather, it would not be difficult to stray off it in mist or snow, with the possibility of wandering off into some of the less hospitable parts of Rannoch Moor. On these hills, to sit down and wait for mist to clear away is an invitation to exposure in any but the mildest weather: the party should have map and compass — and skill in their use.

Across the fine old bridge by Kingshouse Hotel the Way runs north to a T-junction where a signpost points boldly eastwards over the empty moor to 'Rannoch by Loch Laidon'. It is nearly 20 km under the slopes of A'Chruach to Rannoch Station on the West Highland Railway, where the public road from Loch Rannoch ends. There have for decades been proposals to close this gap in the road network of Scotland, but fortunately none has succeeded. A road here would have little intrinsic value as a scenic route: its function would be mainly as an extra link in various tourist circuits, and its construction would substantially erode the unmatched wilderness character of Rannoch Moor.

Here the Way turns left and follows the old Glen Coe road westwards towards its junction with the A82. Directly ahead looms the pyramid of Buachaille Etive Mor, a great bastion between Glen Etive on the left and Glen Coe to the right After almost a kilometre, when the concrete arch of the bridge on the main road is receding to the left, the old military road strikes off over a stile up the hill to the right. You have a choice of two routes from here to Altnafeadh — on the old road under Beinn a'Chrulaiste, or across to the River Coupall and along its banks. The upper route is slightly shorter, gives somewhat easier walking, especially in wet weather, and holds its height to give excellent views to Buachaille Etive Mor and down through Glen Coe. The lower route is further from the main road and brings you close under the cliffs of the Buachaille.

The old military road begins as a rather faint track, but becomes more defined as it climbs on to the slopes of Beinn a'Chrulaiste. Its highest point offers a wild mountain panorama round from the bare moorland rising behind Kingshouse past Meall a'Bhuiridh, Sron na Creise, and Buachaille Etive Mor to the tops of the Three Sisters of Glen Coe. The route then ambles down as a pleasant heathery terrace to Altnafeadh, skirting the main road for the last few hundred metres.

The alternative line continues on the Glen Coe road to the Glen Etive crossroads and along the main road for a short distance before it strikes across to the River Coupall, following its banks up to the footbridge at Lagangarbh, below Altnafeadh. This route has a special attraction for those interested in geology, as it clearly shows a notable structural feature. The 'manie mightie steep hills upon Glen Koen', as Timothy Pont described them, are the product of a remarkable geological phenomenon, the cauldron-subsidence, of which this is the classic example, though similar features underlie Ben Nevis and the mountains round Loch Etive. In the Glen Coe case a ring-fault cut out a great block of lavas of the Lower Old Red Sandstone period, an oval about 14 km by 7 km. The block, in W. H. Murray's vivid image, 'foundered like a loose fitting piston in a cylinder block of Dalradian schist', with molten magma rising around the edges of the sinking lavas to ring and fill the cauldron with granite. Subsequent erosion has carved the mountains out from the original lavas.

At the eastern end of the glen, the precise line of the ring-fault is uncertain, but the margin of the granite is evident. In the bed of the Coupall as the river turns southwards in the wide waterslide down over the moor, banded grey Dalradian strata change over a short distance through a zone of contact into a strong red granite that forms massive slabs in the river-bed.

Both of the optional routes for the Way are dominated by the great crags of Buachaille Etive Mor, which make the mountain one of the finest and most popular rock-climbing peaks in Scotland. Some of the best-known features can be readily identified: the upstanding thumb of the Crowberry Tower below and to the east of the summit, with Crowberry Ridge falling from it; the bulbous bulwark of North Buttress, with steep walls and hard climbs on both its flanks: and the open chasm of Great Gully to its right, with the dark slit of Raven's Gully in its upper part, hard against the buttress. There are easier climbs, but they are not readily found by those unfamiliar with the mountain, and the use of a rope and the SMC *Climber's Guide* are strongly recommended.

For walkers, a relatively straightforward route goes up the corrie behind the SMC hut at Lagangarbh to its head in Coire na Tulaich, from which the ridge can be gained. Even so this is a rough scree scramble at the top and demands an ice axe in winter or spring as well as careful compass work on the ridge in thick weather. A way up or down the Buachaille can also be found in Coire Cloiche Finne above Glen Etive, but again a little care is required. From the top of this fine peak there is a wide vista over the Moor and north to the hump of Ben Nevis beyond the intervening ridges of the Mamores.

In common with most of Glen Coe, the Buachaille is owned and managed by the National Trust for Scotland. This property was the first of the Trust's Mountainous Properties, being purchased between 1935 and 1937 with funds contributed by members of the SMC, the Pilgrim Trust and the general public. Much of the money, as well as the initiative for the purchase, came from Percy Unna, then president of the SMC, who later bequeathed his substantial fortune to the Trust for similar purposes. The management of the Mountainous Properties is generally based on principles recommended by him; he felt strongly that the hills should be left in a 'primitive' condition, and should not be made easier or safer to climb.

In this he showed a remarkable foresight, long before pressures from recreation and tourism presented any real threat to such areas. Unna died in 1950, as the result of a heart attack on Beinn Eunaich near Loch Awe, on the eve of the Hogmanay meet of the SMC. He is buried in Pennyfuir Cemetery, just outside Oban.

Under the Buachaille the riverside route passes the stepping-stones over to Jacksonville, the hut of the famous Creag Dhu Club — access by invitation only — and follows the windings of the Coupall as far as the footbridge on the path down from Altnafeadh to Lagangarbh. The well-equipped hut at Lagangarbh is run by the Scottish Mountaineering Club, and accommodation can be booked by members of clubs affiliated to the Mountaineering Council of Scotland or the British Mountaineering Council.

The Way's two variants meet again on the main road by Altnafeadh: from there the Way strikes uphill by the burn, crosses it, and rejoins the old military road above the Altnafeadh plantation. From here you can look southwest through the remarkable pass of the Lairig Gartain separating the two Buachailles, Mor and Beag. The distinctive shape and profound depth of the valley, with steep slopes swooping nearly 500 metres from the tops on either side, indicate that it has been much eroded by the Rannoch glaciers, but examination of the map will show an extra factor in its formation. It is possible to trace an almost exactly straight line from upper Loch Etive through the Lairig Gartain and Altnafeadh, across the Blackwater Reservoir and far to the north-east under Beinn a'Bhric and Beinn na Lap. This linear feature, a shatter zone associated with a fault, has allowed the forces of erosion to work to greater effect, producing these sharply pronounced landforms.

The section of military road from Altnafeadh over to Kinlochleven has long been known as the Devil's Staircase, though that name is strictly applied only to the carefully engineered zig-zags under the summit on the Rannoch side. From Major Caulfeild's report for 1750 it seems likely, though not absolutely certain, that the Devil's Staircase road was built during that year. Something like 450 officers and men of Rich's and Guise's

Regiments were involved in the work. It seems probable that the troops themselves christened the zig-zags the Devil's Staircase; Roy's Map has the name 'Mam Grianau' on the pass, but that name seems to have passed into obscurity.

The Roy Map, based on survey work between 1748 and 1755, also clearly shows that there was a track of sorts down Glen Coe as well as over the ridge to Kinlochleven. As at the Mam Carraigh above Loch Tulla, the shorter, steeper route dictated by military priorities found little favour, and in 1785 the Staircase and the Lairig Mor road between Kinlochleven and Fort William were abandoned for an improved route by Glen Coe to Ballachulish and along the shore of Loch Linnhe. As a result, the wide and sinuous hairpins of the Staircase proper are reasonably well-preserved, with good kerbing and bottoming in parts. Erosion caused over the years by water, by walkers, and by motor-cycles (this was often a stage in the Scottish Six Days Trial held in May each year) has been sensitively repaired.

There was no proper road here in February 1692, when the infamous Massacre of Glen Coe took place in the lower, inhabited part of the glen. Had there been a road, the Massacre might have been more brutal than it was, since it could have permitted the Government troops to complete their intended cordon of the glen and to prevent the escape of the trapped MacDonalds.

The Massacre was the result of a complex interaction of political forces: between Hanoverians and Jacobites, between Lowlanders and Highlanders, and between rival Highland clans. Anyone interested in the detailed background to the Massacre will find full and readable accounts in John Buchan's *The Massacre of Glencoe* or John Prebble's *Glencoe.* In brief, the MacDonalds of Glen Coe fell foul of the Hanoverian strategy for the pacification of the Highlands, perhaps because they were a small clan with a reputation for reiving and raiding similar to that of the MacGregors. Through loyalty to the exiled James VII, MacIain, the elderly chief of the clan, narrowly failed to take a prescribed oath of allegiance to William III by the deadline set for the end of December 1691. Although more powerful chiefs had failed to take the oath altogether, the ambitious Secretary of State for Scotland, Sir John

Dalrymple, decided to make an example of the MacDonalds. The king, embroiled in a full-scale war with France, gave his approval to measures 'to extirpate that sept of thieves'.

Lochan at the top of the Devil's Staircase.

On 1 February 1692, 120 soldiers of Argyll's Regiment, commanded by Captain Robert Campbell of Glenlyon, were quartered on the people of Glen Coe. Although Glenlyon had suffered losses of property at the hands of MacIain and his men, he was also related to the chief by marriage, and the MacDonalds welcomed the troops into their homes without any suspicion of what was to come.

On 12 February the orders for the massacre reached Fort William from Edinburgh. Lt-Col James Hamilton relayed the command to Campbell at Glen Coe through a detachment under Major Robert Duncanson at Ballachulish, and set off with 400 men to close the escape routes from the glen. Above the head of Loch Leven, however, Hamilton's force encountered a blizzard, and did not reach the upper end of Glen Coe until about 11am on the 13th.

By that time the grisly butchery of the Massacre was all but done. At 5am, in the winter dark, Glenlyon set his troops to fulfil the orders he had received, 'to putt all to the sword under seventy'. MacIain was roused from his bed and shot in the back; his wife was stripped, and her rings torn from her fingers. As the neighbours rose in alarm, they were murdered in their turn. In all about 40 adults were killed, the remainder fleeing to the hills under cover of the blizzard, in which an unknown number more died of exposure and starvation. The thatch of their houses was burned, the livestock driven off and Glen Coe left plundered and empty.

As the news of the Massacre became known throughout Scotland, public feeling rose against its perpetrators. At length, in 1695, a commission of inquiry investigated the outrage; as a result of its findings, Dalrymple lost his Secretaryship. Few others suffered any real retribution. But the memory of the Massacre and revulsion against it have persisted over three centuries: not so much for the scale of its brutality, since clan warfare had generated many atrocities at least as bad, as for its appalling character - a ruthlessly calculated political mass-murder carried out by the trusted guests of the victims.

The last zig-zag of the Staircase leads rightwards to the cairn on the summit, a rather undistinguished ridge of moss and boulders. If you are favoured with clear weather, the view from this highest point of the West Highland Way well repays the climb up. Given time to spare, it is worth climbing the ridge westwards to Stob Mhic Mhartuin for a wider prospect that takes in the rugged peaks on the south side of Glen Coe. For your own safety, however, you should not wander too far off the Way, as the ridge eventually leads to the narrow and difficult traverse of the Aonach Eagach..

The new aspect of this view is to the north, where the Way's final mountain milepost, the ponderous bulk of Ben Nevis, hunches against the crag of its great North-East Buttress. The shapely cone of Carn Mor Dearg provides a foil to Nevis on its right. Ranged in front, the Mamores present a surge of varied peaks and swinging ridges above the deep-cut Leven valley.

The old road pauses a little on the crest, then drops steadily into the bleak, boggy glen to the north, and contours along the spur on its western flank. Before long you catch your first glimpse of the Blackwater dam and reservoir to the north-east. These represent the power source for the aluminium smelter at Kinlochleven, and in a very real sense are the reason for the town's existence.

The dam, nearly a kilometre long and over 25 metres high, was built between 1905 and 1909, and created a reservoir 13 km long where there had previously been only three small lochs in a bleak moorland valley.

Up to 3000 men were employed in building the Blackwater scheme; it was one of the last great engineering projects built by navvies, the tough itinerant manual labourers whose muscle power created the canals and railways of industrial Britain. Tales abound of the hard-working, hard-living, hard-drinking life of the Blackwater navvies; many of the stories are drawn from the pages of the 'autobiographical novel' *Children of the Dead End* by Patrick MacGill, a remarkable self-educated writer and versifier. MacGill vividly describes the risks, squalor and lawlessness that were characteristic of life in the hills above Kinlochleven. He tells, for instance, of gangs of five men working ten-hour shifts on drilling - one man holding the steel drill between his knees while the others struck it with their sledgehammers in rotation:

> '. . . it is really a wonder that more accidents do not take place, especially since the labour is often performed after a heavy night's drinking or gambling. A holder is seldom wounded; when he is struck he dies'.

Materials and supplies were transported to the dam site from Kinlochleven by an overhead rope railway known as the 'blondin' after the famous tightrope walker. It was a favourite ploy with the navvies to find spots where the buckets on the blondin could be reached from the ground with a long pole; then to identify and tip the buckets containing food or beer barrels, and scramble for the proceeds. It is also on record that a pedlar who was keen to trade with the navvies was maliciously induced to ride the blondin up to the dam at the end of a Saturday shift, and spent an unpleasant weekend in a stationary bucket high above the Leven gorge.

The navvies were of course a shifting population, and the movements of individuals - and in some cases, even their names - were unknown to their fellow-workers. During the five years of the construction work, a number of bodies were found in the area of the Devil's Staircase and in the wilds of Rannoch Moor: the remains of those

who had set out for Blackwater and had been caught in bad weather, or of some who had made an expedition to Kingshouse Inn for whisky and lost the path back in darkness, mist or snow.

As the Way rounds the end of the spur and descends to cross the Allt a'Choire Odhair-mhoir, more of the Blackwater works come into view: the culvert carrying the water along the valley flank to the penstock from which it rushes down six great pipes to Kinlochleven, and the access road and power line up to the dam. On the opposite side of the Leven glen you may be able to trace the feeder conduit to Blackwater from Loch Eilde Mor under the eastern tops of the Mamores; this addition to the water catchment was constructed during the 1914—18 War, largely by German prisoner-of-war labour. To the left, steep broken spurs fall northwards from the Aonach Eagach towards the abrupt and massive peak of Garbh Bheinn — well-named 'the rough mountain' — which looms over Kinlochleven.

This is the country through which Robert Louis Stevenson made David Balfour and Alan Breck travel eastwards after the Appin Murder in *Kidnapped*. RLS clearly had a good eye for a rugged landscape setting. On the gradual descent towards the culvert and penstock you will notice the wealth of birchwood clothing the steep slopes of the craggy Leven valley and its tributary glens, a pleasing contrast to the virtually treeless moors you have crossed. These woods are partly the result of the roughness of the ground which makes the young trees less accessible to sheep and deer; but they are also in part an unexpected by-product of the industrial development at Kinlochleven, since it provided an alternative employment for the crofters and shepherds of the area, thus reducing the level of sheep-grazing and allowing the trees to regenerate.

The crest of the spur on which the penstock stands is a dramatic viewpoint with a fine sense of height and depth. From here the pipes carrying the water from the dam plunge down 250 metres in a kilometre — the full head of water is about 300 metres — towards the factory site at Kinlochleven. Deep-set in the glen, a few houses at

Opposite: Walker near Kinlochleven.

Kinlochmore appear in domestic contrast to the surrounding hills that rise 1000 metres in steep broken slopes to rugged ridges. Although Loch Leven itself remains hidden among its flanking mountains, you can trace the line of the West Highland Way under the Mamore slopes and into the Lairigmor pass amidst the hills on the north side of the loch. Even in wild weather this is an atmospheric eyrie.

From the penstock the Way follows the works access road, winding steeply down into Coire Mhorair, crossing the stream beneath the little water supply reservoir, and running down into the gorge of the Leven close above Kinlochleven. It parallels the pipes through the gorge and follows them down to the back of the former aluminium works, where it crosses them and takes a rough road rightwards to a bridge over the river. Hard upstream from the bridge an unmistakable red dyke of igneous rock crosses the river, catching the eye by its colourful contrast with the off-white quartzite on either side. The wall and abutments of the bridge repeat the theme in a chequerboard of red and white stone blocks.

Beyond the bridge, the Way turns left and follows Wade's Road — which ought by rights to be Caulfeild's Road — alongside a housing scheme as far as Morrison Crescent. It then turns left along a riverside path, into the centre of the town where it joins the B863 again by the bridge over the River Leven. Particularly after rain, it is worth taking the few minutes necessary to visit the waterfall on the Allt Coire na Ba: the path turns off Wade's Road just by the Episcopal Church.

Kinlochleven provides the walker with a fair range of shops, cafes and a bank (the first since Drymen). There is also a choice of bed and breakfast accommodation, a hostel, a bunkhouse and a campsite. Kinlochleven is unique in the Highlands as a 'factory town', and has had a curious evolution. In 1769, when Pennant breakfasted here 'on most excellent minced stag, the only form I thought that animal good in', there was only a tiny village on the flats at the head of the loch. By 1900 there were two small settlements, each with a deer-stalking lodge and a couple of cottages: Kinlochbeg on the south side of the river, Kinlochmore on the north.

Then came the aluminium works. Although it had originally been planned to build factory and housing on the north side where more flat ground was available, difficulties with the landowner and tenant of the Mamore estate caused the whole village to be built on the Kinlochbeg side under the lowering bulk of Garbh Bheinn, which kept the settlement entirely in shadow for more than two months in midwinter. Even so, the British Aluminium Company was required to build Mamore Lodge high above the village to maintain the amenity of the Kinlochmore estate; and although small areas north of the river were feued to the Company in 1914, the problem of land for expansion went unsolved until 1935, when the Company bought the entire Mamore estate.

The summit of Devil's Staircase.

New difficulties arose as soon as the first houses went up at Kinlochmore, because the Leven formed the boundary between the counties of Argyll and Inverness. An inquiry in 1928 settled for the status quo, and until reorganisation in 1975 Kinlochleven had to contend with a series of minor problems and complex arrangements over local government, housing, education and medical services. There were even two police stations, one each side of the river, for a population of less than 2000. Offenders in Kinlochbeg were taken to Oban for trial; in Kinlochmore, to Fort William.

Fifteen years after work had begun on the smelter and power scheme, Kinlochleven remained an extremely isolated

place, with road access only by a rough cart-track along
the north side of the loch, and a limited boat service. In
1922, however, the present road on the steep south flank
of Loch Leven was opened, much of the work having
been undertaken by prisoners of war; and in 1927 the
north shore road was substantially improved. For nearly
50 years thereafter the Kinlochleven loop was a useful if
circuitous by-pass for the Ballachulish ferry at the foot of
the loch, when summer tourist traffic congested the crossing, or after the ferry had gone off for the night. However, the opening of the long-awaited Ballachulish bridge
in 1975 removed the necessity to go round the loch, and
Kinlochleven sees much less traffic now.

Recent years have thrust further change upon
Kinlochleven. After a period of decline the smelter has
now closed, and the town is being promoted and developed as a walking and climbing centre, for which it is
well suited. Developments include The Ice Factor, a £3m
indoor climbing centre housed in part of the former
smelter complex. It is open all year.

Loch Leven with snow-covered Mamores in the background.

Houses in Kinlochleven huddled under the mist covered Mamore hills.

Kinlochleven – Fort William

SUMMARY

Distance: 22.5km (14 miles).

Height Range: 50-280m.

Terrain: The last stage of the Way involves a steady climb from Kinlochleven on a good track over the Lairig Mor and another climb through forestry into Glen Nevis, both reaching a height of about 280m and giving fine views of Ben Nevis and surrounding hills. Final short road stretch into Fort William, which has a full range of services for the traveller.

Lochaber

L IKE Lennox and Breadalbane, Lochaber is one of the ancient provinces of Scotland. Traditionally, Lochaber is considered to have included all the country north from Loch Leven to the Spean valley on the east side of the Great Glen, and the region between Loch Eil and Glen Garry, right to the west coast, on the west side of the Great Glen. For our purposes the West Highland Way enters the Lochaber area at Kinlochleven, and proceeds through a typical range of its scenery - high mountains dissected by deep valleys, bare upper glens and hill lochs, with sea-lochs reaching far into the interior - to the centre at Fort William.

The hub of the province also provided its name, for Lochaber is thought to mean simply 'the loch estuary', and thus to refer specifically to Inverlochy, close by the modern town of Fort William. This strategic centre controls a major cross-roads where the Great Glen meets Loch Eil, giving access to the west, and the Spean valley, linking eastwards to Badenoch and Strathspey. Its military significance was acknowledged at least as early as the 13th century, by the building of Inverlochy Castle, later supplanted by successive garrisons at Fort William. From this central strongpoint, Cromwellian and Hanoverian troops sought to control the powerful Jacobite clans of Lochaber, the Camerons and various septs of MacDonald.

Evolving lines of communication also tended to focus on this area: the Caledonian Canal and the steamer routes in the 19th century; the military roads and their modern replacements; the West Highland railway and its spur lines to Mallaig and Fort Augustus. Fort William and its satellite towns on the Inverlochy flats have thus developed into one of the main commercial and industrial centres in the Highlands. Their combined population of over 13,000 is second only to Inverness.

Kinlochleven — Lundavra
(12 km; 7.5 miles)

THE last leg of the West Highland Way from Kinlochleven to Fort William is 22.5 km long. It divides naturally into two almost equal parts, the break point occurring at Blar a'Chaorainn, near Lundavra, where the Way leaves the Caulfeild road to cross into Glen Nevis. The path from Kinlochleven to that point follows the military road the whole way, and generally gives excellent walking. It climbs sharply out of the Loch Leven valley to about 250 metres and rises gradually thereafter to the summit of the Lairigmor, 'the great pass', at a little over 330 metres. There is not much chance of going astray, but once again there is little shelter to be had on the higher part of this walk, and wind and rain funnelled through the pass may make life thoroughly unpleasant unless you are equipped to withstand those conditions.

The Way takes the B863 road as far as the north-western edge of Kinlochleven, branching off opposite the school to pass behind the filling station on the north side of the road. On this first stretch there are some clear remnants of the original road construction; the stone bottoming on the fords is particularly well preserved. The path climbs steadily through the birchwoods, with backward glimpses of the loch below. Gradually Kinlochleven begins to recede into its cranny deep-set among the hills, and Loch Leven takes on its true fiord-like character. Westwards, the shapely cone of the Pap of Glencoe - Sgorr na Ciche in Gaelic - stands proud above the loch.

The path forks a short distance below the access road up to Mamore Lodge. The Way takes the leftwards line, crosses the road, and climbs steeply up by the old road beyond, here in a rough gravelly trench. After a few hundred metres, the path crosses a little woodland stream and rejoins the military road coming up from the lochside road; from there on to its junction with the Lairigmor track, it is excellently graded and drained. Although the climb is a steady one, there are one or two splendid open viewpoints that will offer a ready excuse for a rest and a reward for your effort. To the west the view down the loch is closed by the Pap and the rugged, knobbly spurs of

Beinn a'Bheithir (Ben Vair) behind Ballachulish. To the south, broken and gully-scored slopes rise to the high pinnacled crest of the Aonach Eagach, the north wall of Glen Coe. This aptly-named 'notched ridge' provides a superb airy traverse that can be thoroughly recommended to those with experience of mountain scrambling. Eastwards the line of the Way can be traced down round the spurs below the Devil's Staircase into the Leven glen, giving an encouraging sense of the distance that has been covered.

Once you have reached the Lairigmor track that comes along the hill-front from Mamore Lodge you have done most of the work, and the walking is easy, though the track does rise and fall a little. You are now, as Pennant put it, 'on the side of a hill, an aweful height above Loch-Leven'. However, once the last pines in the steep-sided gorge of the Allt Nathrach are left behind, the character of the route changes. The bare hill-slopes on either hand rise to enclose the glen and limit the view; the track pursues a rather lonely course onwards to the pass, with only a line of power poles for company. Particularly in wet or misty weather, the Lairigmor can be a bleak place.

In fine weather, outwith the stalking season from August to October, the hills on either flank offer very attractive options or additions to the crossing of the pass. On the south the ridge of Beinn na Caillich and Mam na Gualainn provides a magnificent belvedere above Loch Leven; on the north, the Mamore ridge gives some of Scotland's best high-level ridge walking, and enthusiasts can achieve a strenuous grand climax to the West Highland Way by taking a route over the ridge into the middle section of Glen Nevis. The SMC *Central Highlands Guide* provides all the necessary detail of the terrain and possible routes.

Both of these ranges have an added advantage for walkers in being readily accessible by good stalkers' tracks. These excellent paths are in most cases a remnant of the late-Victorian heyday of the deer forest and stalking. In those days labour was plentiful and cheap, and estates with large staffs had the manpower to construct great networks of paths. They were very carefully graded, sometimes with long series of zig-zags on steep slopes, for the ponies used to bring down the stags at the end of the day, and skilfully drained to prevent their erosion by water. Their continued existence, usually after decades of minimal maintenance, is a silent tribute to their builders.

The summit of the Lairigmor is an unspectacular flat col; since the glen turns northwards a few kilometres further west, there is no great revelation of a new landscape, but only a prospect of the wide glen stretching ahead. The Way descends gently past the house of Tigh-na-sleubhaich, 'the house by the gullied slope', to Lairigmor itself, a sad ruin. From here, an old path goes off leftwards across the face of Mam na Gualainn and over the ridge to Callert on Loch Leven. This path connected the Lairigmor road to the Glen Coe road when there was a ferry across the loch to Invercoe.

The Way rounds the granite, gully-seamed spur of Meall a'Chaorainn and continues its gradual descent, but now to the northwards. In this part of the glen the crofters around Blarmachfoldach had their summer shielings, and traces of the simple stone huts can be found by the burns that cross the Way. The cattle would be brought up here to graze for eight weeks or so in high summer, and were usually tended by young folk, women and children, while the men worked the croft. Although conditions at the shielings must have been primitive, in general the Highlanders of old seem to have looked forward to the 'flitting' to the shieling as a holiday.

The glen is still grazed, though now mainly by sheep, and salt-licks at intervals by the side of the road are intended to supplement the meagre mineral content of the acidic soil in the area. There is a sheep-fank at the southern edge of the Forestry Commission plantation. Once the Way leaves this plantation, you will catch glimpses over to the left of Lochan Lunn Da Bhra, a pleasant little loch with a few pines around its shores. The name is somewhat obscure, but may be a corruption of a Gaelic compound meaning 'the castle in the water'.

Local tradition avers that Macbeth died in a castle on an island in the loch, but in fact he was killed by Malcolm III in Aberdeenshire. The loch is also supposed to have been the haunt of a 'waterbull', a malicious mythical beast which would emerge from the loch and drag other cattle in to drown. This is a variant on the Celtic tradition of the

kelpie or water-horse which lured young men to mount it – or, in some accounts, merely to stroke it. They were then unable to detach themselves from the beast, which would charge off into the loch with them. The mangled remains of the victim would reappear some time later.

At the information shelter at the northern end of the plantation, a short distance from the derelict house of Blar a'Chaorainn, the Way and the old military road, close companions since Glen Falloch, finally part company. The Way takes to the hill again as a last fling on its crossing into Glen Nevis. The military road, as a single-track tarmac road, rambles up and down past the crofts of Blarmachfoldach and Glengour before descending steeply down into the suburbs of Fort William above Ach'an Todhair (Achintore), and thence to the southern end of the High Street in the town (7.25 km; 4.5 miles).

As a route this road is not without attractions of its own, including a wide prospect of the head of Loch Linnhe, with Fort William and its sprawling satellite settlements at Inverlochy, Caol and Corpach. It will have a particular appeal as an easier option for the weary or weather-beaten. Those favoured with fair weather, and still feeling fit, will probably prefer to take the more scenic and more satisfying route through to Glen Nevis.

Lundavra — Fort William
(10.5 km; 6.5 miles)

THE final stretch of the Way gives rough walking through the forestry plantations to the head of the valley behind Blarmachfoldach; a sharp descent into Glen Nevis is followed by a gentle concluding walk on forest tracks and public road to the edge of Fort William, where the Way ends near all the amenities, services and transport facilities of a major regional centre. The crossing to Glen Nevis offers excellent views of Ben Nevis at close quarters, and few who see the mountain from here in clear weather will be able to resist the temptation to climb it as a grand finale to the Way.

The West Highland Way branches off the old military road just inside the forest gates at Blar a'Chaorainn, and climbs rightwards beneath the power lines into a narrow

Previous page: Lochan Lunn da Bhra.

break between the spruces. In places the path follows the old head-dyke, and accompanies it through the trees and over intervening stretches of open ground towards the head of the glen. This is the old head-dyke marking the upper limit of improved ground around the settlements in the glen, and separating it from the rough grazing on the mountain slopes. The dyke is at an unusually high altitude for this part of Scotland, partly because of topography and partly because of the underlying geology. The glen enjoys a southerly aspect, but is fairly sheltered from the prevailing south-westerly winds; and the rock formation beneath is the Ballachulish limestone, which helps to give a more fertile soil in a region where leaching by heavy rainfall tends to produce very acidic soils. Thus in the 18th century there were three farming townships in the glen here, at Blarmachfoldach, Blar a'Chaorainn, and Tollie, with a combined population of perhaps 200 in 1812. Today only a few crofts are worked at Blarmachfoldach; there are only ruins at Blar a'Chaorainn; and the remaining stones of Tollie, above the north bank of the Allt nan Gleannan, are vanishing beneath the Sitka spruce.

The Way enjoys an interlude of open ground, where it climbs over a viewpoint knoll above a former melt-water channel, before it goes back into the plantations, turning northeastwards towards the head of the glen. Beyond the rough slopes of Sgorr Chalum on the right, the mighty form of Ben Nevis, scarred by deep-cut gullies, begins to loom ahead. This is the south-western aspect of the mountain, the slopes that overlook Glen Nevis. The path to the summit follows roughly the left skyline from the col with Meall an t-Suidhe. Few would claim that the Ben looks shapely from this direction, but it impresses by its sheer bulk.

In the middle ground, the knobbly ridge-crest above Glen Nevis is of more immediate interest. The West Highland Way does not take the more obvious col under Sgorr Chalum; it descends a little to cross the long nameless stream running down off the spur of Mullach nan Coirean from the right, and contours roughly midway up the forested slope above the flats of the Allt nan Gleannan. It then breaks from the line of the dyke, and cuts leftwards across the head of the flats under the hill of Dun Deardail before climbing steeply up to the col northwest of the hill.

Dun Deardail is an ancient vitrified fort, dating back to the Iron Age. Its elevated site has led some writers to suggest that it formed one of a chain of watchtowers from Oban to Strathpeffer, but it is difficult to trace any such chain, or to conceive of a plausible function for it. It seems more likely that the high hilltop site was simply the best defensive position available in the area. The rubble walls of the Dun, now largely grassed over, were vitrified - fused into a glassy matrix - by fire. Vitrified forts are found so widely that it was for long felt that vitrification was a deliberate technique employed to strengthen the ramparts of the fort, but the many unburnt timbers which survive argue strongly against this. Archaeologists now assume that the process occurred accidentally when the timber work lacing or fronting the masonry of the fort was burned by attackers.

The etymology of the fort's name is doubtful; it does not appear on early maps. Some authors connect it with Deirdre, the legendary Celtic princess, but others translate it as 'the fort on the stormy hill', which has a more convincing ring to it.

At the top of the slope, the Way turns north and traverses over the col, with dramatic views of the Ben above, before dropping down onto an excellent forest road. The Way turns left along this road and begins a gentle, sidling descent into Glen Nevis. The harder walking on the Way is now behind you, and the view ahead, over the campsite and farmland of lower Glen Nevis, opens out to the wide lowland floor of the Great Glen around Inverlochy. Journey's end is in sight.

After 1.5 km or so, a branch road cuts back down to the right. The final spur off the West Highland Way, leading down to accommodation and service facilities in the glen, follows this road, turns down to the left, and crosses the flats to the public road by the River Nevis. Much of the valley floor is given over to a large camping and caravan site which in summer is a scene of colourful bustle and activity. A short distance up the glen road, this branch of the Way ends at the Youth Hostel, a large wooden building by the road.

Glen Nevis itself merits a day or two for exploration. From various higher points in the valley the Mamore tops appear to great advantage. It is ironic that from

Kinlochleven on, the Way runs so close to them that their full height and shapeliness are not readily appreciated. Sgurr a'Mhaim and Stob Ban - 'the white top' from its quartzite capping - form an effective backdrop to the lower part of the glen. However, the true glories of Glen Nevis are found in its mid-section, from Achriabhach to Steall, hard under the southern flank of Ben Nevis where mountain, river and woodland scenery blend in wild grandeur. Even in wet weather that piece of country is an exhilarating experience.

The Way proper continues on the forest road through the plantations for another 600 metres or so, then turns sharp right off the track and heads down to the public road in the glen, meeting it near a convenient car-park and picnic site. On the left it passes close by a tree-covered knoll, the old cemetery of the sept of Clan Cameron who inhabited Glen Nevis. The last 2.25 km of the Way follows the pavement by the road above the river. About 800 metres along this stretch the route passes a big erratic boulder known as Clach Comhairle, 'the stone of counsel', to which various stories are attached. The Victorian author of a local history took a sardonic view of one of these tales:

> 'The auld wives say that on a certain night of the year (the exact date they keep to themselves, for obvious reasons) the boulder turns round three times, and that any one fortunate enough to find it on the move will get answers to any three questions he may put before it finally settles to rest again. I am sorry I am unable to vouch for the truth of this legend from personal experience. Many a time and oft, by day and by night, have I passed this venerable relic, and have even had the reckless audacity to knock out my pipe ashes on its moss-covered surface; but it has never honoured me with so much as a tremor.'

On its last westwards stretch the surroundings of the Way become gradually more domestic and suburban. The route ends at Bridge of Nevis, in summer a congested junction where tourist traffic to Glen Nevis competes with commercial traffic on the A82 road north. From here it is only a short walk to the transport facilities, shops and accommodation of Fort William's bustling town centre.

The town has a markedly diverse character; it is regional service centre, industrial town, and tourist resort. Virtually no trace remains of its main historic function, though its by-name in Gaelic is still *An Gearasdan* (the garrison) and in English 'The Fort'. If you have time to spare, a visit to the West Highland Museum off the High Street can be recommended, both for its intrinsic interest, and as further background to your walk on the West Highland Way.

The ascent of Ben Nevis has already been suggested as a fitting grand finale to the Way. The old pony track to the summit starts from Achintee, 2 km up from Bridge of Nevis on the east side of the River Nevis; there are footbridges across the river from the car park opposite Achintee, and from the Youth Hostel in the glen. Normal time is about 3 1/2 hours for the ascent, and something over two hours for the descent, but the advice given by the minister of Kilmallie Parish in the Old Statistical Account remains sound:

> 'Few can perform a journey to the top of Benevis, and make proper observations, going and returning, in less than 7 hours; and still fewer, without feeling, in their limbs, the effects of the fatigue, for a day or two after.'

When he was writing, in 1793, it was not yet certain that Nevis was the highest point in Britain. Ben MacDui, highest of the Cairngorm tops, was known to be of similar height, and the question was not resolved in Nevis' favour until the early 19th century. The record for the annual Ben Nevis Race, usually held on the first Saturday in September, is under 90 minutes up and down – a remarkable time by any standards.

Bear in mind that weather conditions on the summit are frequently dramatically different from those in the valley, and equip yourself accordingly. The Achintee route climbs gently on the bouldery track from the old farm; the route from the Youth Hostel crosses the bridge opposite the hostel and climbs steeply to join the old pony-track. This has suffered from the passage of countless feet, particularly where descending walkers have cut the corners of the zig-zags. To help minimise further erosion

Opposite: Ben Nevis in winter.

you should follow the path round and get the benefit of its easy gradients. The path was built at a total cost of £800, to serve the meteorological observatory which operated on top of the Ben from 1883 to 1904; at the turn of the century walkers were required to make a small contribution towards its maintenance. In recent years, large sums have been spent on repairing and restoring the path, and in some places it has been directed along an easier line.

The path leads round into the valley of the Red Burn and on to the col behind Meall an t-Suidhe. The upper part of the route zig-zags up long boulder slopes, which can seem interminable unless compensation can be found in the ever-widening view or in observing the local geology. Nevis is another cauldron subsidence like Glen Coe, but a double one. The summit rocks consist of lavas representing the roof of a first, subterranean subsidence that collapsed into a second cauldron. The inner granite ring of the cauldron underlies the slope above Meall an t-Suidhe and is acknowledged by the predominance of Carn Dearg hill-names right round the Ben - Carn Dearg being 'the red cairn'.

The true character of Ben Nevis does not reveal itself until the summit is reached. From the edge of its broad plateau a confusion of steep rock ridges, buttresses, ribs and walls drop 600 metres north-eastwards to the Allt a'Mhuillin glen in one of Britain's greatest cliffs. In winter or spring, great cornices of snow and ice project over gully-heads and rock walls, and you will do well to give them a wide berth. Scores of good climbing routes have been forced up these cliffs in a century of mountaineering in summer and winter; there is a special pleasure, your own toil accomplished, in watching the slow upwards progress of a roped party on ridge or buttress.

In good visibility the wider view from Ben Nevis is vast, though it inevitably has a somewhat flattened perspective, being above rather than among the surrounding hills. A small-scale map of Scotland can be useful to identify more distant ranges.

Way-walkers can now look southwards complacently to where their route is marked by its mountain mileposts, and allow themselves a little well deserved self-congratulation.

Appendix I

Select Bibliography

The West Highland Way has a vast background literature. This Bibliography is not a complete list of the references in the text of the guide; it is merely a very small selection of some of the most interesting and useful sources relating to the country around the Way. Many of the books listed below contain comprehensive bibliographies which can be consulted by walkers with specialised interests.

Hill-walking and Mountaineering

Bennet, Donald (1991) The Southern Highlands. 3rd ed. Scottish Mountaineering Trust.

Hodgkiss, Peter (1992) The Central Highlands. 5th ed. SMT.

Murray, W. H. (1987) Scotland's Mountains. SMT.

Brooker, W. D. (ed, 1988). A Century of Scottish Mountaineering. SMT.

Crocket, Ken (1990). Ben Nevis. SMT.

Bennet, Donald (ed, 1991). The Munros. SMT.

Bennet, Donald, Brown, Hamish and Johnstone, Scott (eds, 1992). The Corbetts. SMT.

Drummond, Peter (1991) Scottish Hill and Mountain Names. SMT.

Langmuir, Eric (1984) Mountaincraft and Leadership. British Mountaineering Council.

Geology and Geography

Craig, G. Y. (ed,1983) Geology of Scotland. 2nd ed. Scottish Academic Press.

Edlin, H. L. (ed, 1973) Queen Elizabeth Forest Park Guide: Ben Lomond, Loch Ard and the Trossachs. HMSO.

Manley, Gordon (1962) Climate and the British Scene. Collins Fontana.

O'Dell, A. C. and Walton, K. (1962) The Highlands and Islands of Scotland. Nelson.

Price, Robert (1991) Highland Landforms. Aberdeen University Press.

Sissons, J. B. (1967) The Evolution of Scotland's Scenery. Oliver and Boyd.

Whittow, J. B. (1977) Geology and Scenery in Scotland. Penguin.

Brown, M. and Mendum, J. (1995) Loch Lomond to Stirling – a Landscape Fashioned by Geology. SNH.

Natural History

Bennett, L. (1989) A Guide to the Nature Reserves of Scotland.   Macmillan.

Darling, Frank Fraser and Boyd, J. M. (1964) The Highlands and Islands. Collins.

Nethersole-Thompson, Desmond (1974) Highland Birds. 2nd ed. Highlands and Islands Development Board.

Pearsall, W. H. (1968) Mountains and Moorlands. 2nd ed. Collins Fontana.

Ratcliffe, Derek (1977) Highland Flora. Highlands and Islands Development Board.

Stephen, David (1974) Highland Animals. Highlands and Islands Development Board.

University of Glasgow (1974) A Natural History of Loch Lomond. University of Glasgow Press.

Human History

Buchan, John (1933) The Massacre of Glencoe. Peter Davies.

Gillies, William A. (1980) In Famed Breadalbane: the story of the antiquities, lands and people of a highland district. 2nd ed. Clunie Press.

Kilgour, W. T. (1910). Twenty Years on Ben Nevis (the story of the Observatory). Ernest Press.

Murray, W. H. (1993) Rob Roy MacGregor: his life and times. Canongate Press.

Prebble, John (1966) Glencoe: the Story of the Massacre. Penguin.

Smith, John Guthrie (1886) The Parish of Strathblane and its inhabitants from early times: a chapter in Lennox history. James Maclehose & Sons.

Smith, John Guthrie (1896) Strathendrick and its inhabitants from early times. James Maclehose & Sons.

Roads and Railways

Ang, T. and Pollard, M. (1984) Walking the Scottish Highlands: General Wade's Military Roads. Deutsch.

Haldane, A. R. B. (1971) The Drove Roads of Scotland. 2nd ed. Edinburgh University Press.

Haldane, A. R. B. (1973). New Ways Through the Glens. David & Charles.

Taylor, William (1976) The Military Roads in Scotland. David and Charles.

Thomas, John (1966) The Callander and Oban Railway. David and Charles.

Thomas, John (1970) The West Highland Railway. 2nd ed. Pan.

Novels and Travels

Munro, Neil. John Splendid: the tale of a poor gentleman and the little wars of Lorn. Any edition.

Munro, Neil. The New Road. Any edition.

Murray, Sarah (1982) A companion and useful guide to the beauties of Scotland, edited by W. F. Laughlan. Byway Books.

Scott, Sir Walter. Rob Roy. Any edition.

Stevenson, Robert Louis. Kidnapped. Any edition.

Wordsworth, Dorothy (1974) Recollections of a tour made in Scotland A.D. 1803, edited by J. C. Shairp. James Thin.

Appendix II

Gaelic Place Names

Gaelic place-names are found along the entire length of the West Highland Way, though in some places they have been corrupted and anglicised almost beyond recognition. In the guide the spelling used on the 1:50,000 Ordnance Survey map has been followed for the sake of consistency, though the map-makers themselves have not always achieved a successful resolution between local usage, anglicised forms, and pure Gaelic. Thus the map has Achallader Farm under Beinn Achaladair; Beinglas Farm by the Ben Glas Burn; and Beinn Dubhchraig close by Ben Oss and Ben Lui. No attempt has been made to reproduce Gaelic accentuation in the guide.

Rather than give a long list of place-name meanings of which a good proportion will be doubtful in varying degrees, this appendix provides a short glossary of place-name elements, which should help you to decipher some of the commoner topographical names along the Way for yourself. The Scottish Mountaineering Club's District Guides includes full glossaries of mountain names, and their excellent publication *Scottish Hill and Mountain Names* by Peter Drummond can be thoroughly recommended.

The definite article in Gaelic is highly variable according to the gender, form, and case of the noun. In the nominative it may be *an, am* or *an t-* (masculine), *a', an,* or *an t-* (feminine) or *na, na h-* (plural). In the genitive—'of the'—it may be *a', an, an t-; na, na h-;* and *nan, nam,* respectively. Nouns also change in the genitive: thus *buirich,* 'roaring' or 'bellowing', but *Meall a'Bhuiridh,* 'hill of roaring'. And adjectives follow suit; *Coire Odhar Beag,* 'the small dun-coloured corrie', becomes *Sron a'Choire Odhair-bhig,* 'the spur of the small dun-coloured corrie'. The pronunciation changes too, but that is another story! Anglicised forms are shown in brackets.

ach, achadh (auch)	field
allt	burn, stream
aonach	ridge or moor
ard, aird	height, promontory
baile (bal- or ball-)	hamlet, homestead
ban	fair, white
beag (beg)	little
bealach	pass
beinn (ben)	mountain
beithe	birch
bidean	pinnacle
binnean	small peaked mountain
bo	cow
breac (breck)	speckled
buachaille	herdsman
buidhe	yellow
buirich	roaring, bellowing
cailleach	nun, old woman
caisteal	castle
caol, caolas (kyle)	narrow, strait, firth, kyle
caorann	rowan tree
carn	heap of stones, round rocky hill
carraig	rock
ceann (kin)	head, headland
clach	stone
clachan	hamlet
cnap	hillock
coille	wood, forest
coinneach	moss
coire (corrie)	a round hollow in the mountainside; cirque; sea-gulf, whirlpool
creag (craig)	crag, rock, cliff
crom	crooked
cruach	heap, stack, bold hill
cuil	nook, recess
cul	back, hill-back
damh	ox, stag
darach	oak
dearg	red
dobhran (dorain)	otter
doire (derry)	grove
druim (drum)	the back, a ridge
dubh	black
dun (dum)	fortress, castle, heap, mound
each	horse
eag	notch
eas	waterfall
eilean	island
eun	bird

fada	long
fionn	white, holy
fitheach	raven
fuar	cold
fuaran	well, spring
gabhar	goat
garbh	rough
geal	white
giubhas	fir
glas	grey, green
gleann	narrow valley, glen
gorm	green, blue
guala, gualainn	shoulder of a hill
inbhir (inver)	confluence
inis	(1) island; (2) meadow by river; (3) resting place for cattle
iolair	eagle
iubhair	yew
lagan	little hollow
lairig	a pass
laoigh (lui)	calf
leac (leck)	flat stone, slab
leacach	stony slope
leathad	slope, brae
leitir (letter)	slope, side of a hill
loch, lochan	lake; small lake
mam	large, round or gently rising hill; pass
maol	bare top
mheadhoin (vane)	middle
meall	a round hill
mor	large, great
muileann	mill
mullach	top, summit
nead (nid)	nest
odhar (our)	dun-coloured
righ	king
ros	promontory, wood
ruadh	red, brown
ruighe	slope, run for cattle, shieling
sgorr, sgurr	rocky peak
sron	nose, point, spur
stob	point
stuc	peak
suidhe	seat; level shelf on hillside
tairbeart (tarbet)	portage, isthmus
tigh	house
tulach	knoll, hillock
uisge	water, river

Appendix III

Other Long Distance Walks in Scotland

Readers may be interested in other opportunities for long distance walking in Scotland. A network is steadily growing through development by Scottish Natural heritage, local authorities, tourist boards and enterprise companies. Some of the routes currently open are listed below.

The **Southern Upland Way** crosses southern Scotland from coast to coast, running from Portpatrick, near Stranraer, east to Cockburnspath in Berwickshire, a distance of 340km/212 miles. The route is waymarked with the same symbol of a thistle inside a hexagon as the West Highland Way, and its maintenance is similarly supported by SNH.

The official trail guide, with special route maps, is published by Mercat Press. Other guides are published by Constable and Aurum Press. A free trail leaflet and accommodation and facilities guide can be obtained from Countryside Ranger Service, Scottish Borders Council, Harestanes Visitor Centre, Ancrum, Jedburgh, Scotland TD8 6UQ (tel/fax 01835 830281). Route details from the Scottish Borders Tourist Board site on *www.scot-borders.co.uk* or from *www.dumgal.gov.uk/southernuplandway.*

The route runs from Portpatrick on the west coast of Scotland, not far from Stranraer, to Cockburnspath on the Berwickshire coast south of Dunbar. It passes through a great variety of scenery and reaches its high point at over 700m on Lowther Hill above Wanlockhead. It is a demanding and strenuous route, crossing the grain of the land for much of the way. Highlights include Glen Trool, Wanlockhead (Scotland's highest village), St Mary's Loch and the ancient track over Minch Moor past the tall Three Brethren cairns.

The **Speyside Way** has recently been extended, and now runs for 105km/66 miles from Buckie to Aviemore. It too is waymarked with the thistle inside a hexagon. There is no guidebook at present, but route leaflets can be obtained from Moray Council Ranger Service, Boat of Fiddich, Craigellachie, Aberlour, Scotland AB38 9RQ (tel 01340 881266) and there is a Harveys strip-map of the route. The trail website is at *www.moray.org/area/speyway/ webpages/swhome.htm*

The Speyside Way starts at Buckie on the Morayshire coast and runs west to Spey Bay. It then largely follows the River Spey upriver to Aviemore. Part of the route is on an old railway line. Highlights include Telford's superb bridge at Craigellachie, several distilleries which can be visited, and the views to the Cairngorm hills. A spur route runs inland from Ballindalloch to an alternative terminus in Tomintoul.

The **St Cuthbert's Way** path is a new route, opened in 1996. It runs from Melrose, in the Scottish Borders, to Holy Island, off the Northumberland coast, linking places associated with the life of the seventh century bishop, St Cuthbert. The route is 100km/62 miles long, and is waymarked with the symbol of St Cuthbert's Cross.

The official trail guide, with special Harvey map, is published by Mercat Press. The route map is available separately, printed on waterproof paper. A trail leaflet is available free from Scottish Borders Tourist Board, Shepherd's Mill, Whinfield Road, Selkirk, Scotland TD7 5DT (tel 0870 608 0404, email: *info@scot-borders.co.uk*). Route details can be found on *www.scot-borders.co.uk* or *www.stcuthbertsway.fsnet.co.uk.*

A true cross-Border trail, this walk links a number of places associated with St Cuthbert, who started his ministry at Melrose in the mid 7th century AD and ended it at Lindisfarne, the Holy Island of the Northumberland coast. The walk starts at the superb ruin of Melrose Abbey and climbs to cross the Eildon Hills, before joining the River Tweed. Other highlights include the Roman Road Dere Street, the Cheviot foothills, St Cuthbert's Cave and the crossing of the sands to Lindisfarne.

The **Fife Coastal Path,** linking the four great bridges crossing the Forth and Tay at Queensferry and Dundee was due to be completed during 2002. There is no full guidebook. Leaflets covering the different sections now open are available from Tourist Information Centre, 19

Whytescauseway, Kirkcaldy, Scotland KY1 1XF (tel 01592 267775). Route details from the trail website on *www.fifecoastalpath.co.uk*.

The Fife Coastal Path provides a walk of considerable attraction and variety, with excellent birdlife and a large number of historic sites, museums and interesting towns and villages. The route has particularly good public transport links by bus and train, making linear walks along sections of it easy to arrange.

The **Formartine and Buchan Way** is a footpath and cycleway following disused railway lines in Aberdeenshire from Dyce Station, north of Aberdeen, to twin northern termini at Fraserburgh and Peterhead, a distance of about 65km/40miles. There is no full guidebook, but route leaflets are available from Aberdeen & Grampian Tourist Board, 27 Albyn Place, Aberdeen AB10 1YL (01224 632727), and there is a trail website: *www.buchan.org.uk/ stricfbw.htm*.

The **Great Glen Way** was opened in April 2002. It runs from Fort William (the northern end of the West Highland Way) to the Highlands 'capital', Inverness, generally following the line of the Caledonian Canal and Lochs Lochy, Oich and Ness, a distance of 110km/69 miles. Further information can be obtained from the Tourist Information Centre in Fort William (01397 703781, email: *fortwilliam@host.co.uk*). There are also details of the route on *www.easyways.com/ggwrmap.html*.

Appendix IV

The West Highland Way Race

There is a long-distance race run along the entire length of the West Highland Way and usually held on the third Saturday in June, starting at 3 am in Milngavie. Entries have to be in to the race organiser, Dario Melaragni, by the end of February. E-mail: *westhighlandway.race@virgin.net*, website: *www.whw.zzn.com*. The website includes some details on the West Highland Way which may be useful to walkers, as well as a history of the race.

Men's record holder: Dave Wallace of Balerno, who completed the race in 15 hrs 25 mins (1989). This record was made on the old course, which was shorter than the present West Highland Way. The men's record holder for the new, longer course is Mick Francis of Forres, with a time of 16 hrs 38 mins (1992).

Women's record holder: Kate Jenkins (Carnethy Club, Edinburgh), 18 hrs 52 mins (1999).

Index

Note: Page references in italic Roman numerals refer to the introductory pages of the guide.